VIETNAM GRAFFITI

Messages from a Forgotten Troopship

BY ART & LEE BELTRONE

HOWELL PRESS, INC.
Charlottesville, Virginia

Designed by Dara Powers Parker

Library of Congress Cataloging-in-Publication Data

Beltrone, Art, 1941-
    Vietnam graffiti : messages from a forgotten troopship / by Art & Lee Beltrone.
        p. cm.
    Includes index.
    ISBN 1-57427-154-7
    1. General Nelson M. Walker (Ship)—History. 2. Transports—United States—History—20th century. 3. Vietnamese Conflict, 1961-1975—Graffiti. 4. Vietnamese Conflict, 1961-1975—Collectibles. I. Beltrone, Lee, 1942- II. Title.
        VA65.G456B45 2004
        959.704'345—dc22

                                                    2004019211

ISBN 1-57427-154-7

13 12 11 10 09 08 07 06 05 04
10 9 8 7 6 5 4 3 2 1

Printed in Hong Kong

Howell Press, Inc.
1125 Stoney Ridge Road, Suite A
Charlottesville, VA 22902
(434) 977-4006
www.howellpress.com

TABLE OF CONTENTS

FOREWORD

The *General Nelson M. Walker* troopship was commissioned April 24, 1945, to transport men to and from the battlefields of Europe and Asia. It served during the waning days of World War II, as well as in the Korean and Vietnam wars. No longer active, this massive ship has a resting place today among the other vessels of the "Ghost Fleet" moored in a federal facility on the James River in Virginia. It remains remarkably intact.

In *Vietnam Graffiti: Messages from a Forgotten Troopship*, Art and Lee Beltrone tell the truly fascinating story of the *Walker* and its men. Carrying more than 5,000 troops at a time, the ship was a veritable small town in which all the needs of its enlisted men were addressed, however confined and crowded the space that they inhabited. Through the Beltrones' meticulous research and the animated account contained in this volume, life on the now silent vessel pulses with renewed vitality.

During the Vietnam era the men for whom the *General Nelson M. Walker* was a temporary home left records of their life together on the troopship through lively handwritten inscriptions, slogans, and drawings on the surfaces of the canvas bunk inserts of the bunks under which they slept. Now graying and soiled, hundreds of such reminiscences survive on the *Walker*, evincing the personal thoughts, concerns, and emotions of the young men—often not much more than boys—who inscribed them. Here are memories of home and loved ones, brash statements of bravado and determination in the face of conflict, expressions of fear and anxiety on the approach to the theaters of war, patriotic sentiments, humorous cartoons, and a variety of sexual references.

As with people in any form of confinement, the men of the *Walker* found an outlet for themselves in recording these inscriptions, as well as a relief from oppressive boredom. Many of the drawings are crude, others more accomplished, some showing true skill in execution. But all of them are authentic expressions of self. They are messages from another time in our history, but they are no less resonant today, when young men and women still don military uniforms to defend American interests in distant places.

As director of the American Folk Art Museum in New York City, I am aware that artistic expression often occurs where it is least expected. Through this intriguing volume, Art and Lee Beltrone have recaptured a lost chapter in American military history, while preserving examples of the creativity of the young servicemen who left messages on their way to Vietnam. They speak to us still.

—Gerard C. Wertkin, Director
American Folk Art Museum
New York, New York

ACKNOWLEDGMENTS

I am most grateful to Jack Fisk, my Keswick, Virginia, neighbor and motion picture production designer, for his invitation to accompany him on a working trip to the World War II veteran troopship *General Nelson M. Walker*. That chance visit became the catalyst for this book, and ultimately resulted in the museum preservation of hundreds of historic Vietnam War artifacts salvaged from the ship.

Assistance from many people ensured this would happen.

History-minded Maritime Administration personnel at the James River Reserve Fleet, especially Superintendents Capt. Paul Smith and Mike Bagley, and Mike's deputy, Bob Rohr, made visits possible. At the administration's Washington headquarters, both Eugene J. Magee and Peter Wagner shared the ship's historical records. John Shaw served as our guide during numerous visits to the *Walker*, and prevented our getting "lost" in some remote berthing compartment of the ship.

Staff members at the National Archives in Washington, D.C., as always, were most helpful by locating records needed for research.

World War II crew members Clayton Boyce, Earl W. Day, and Edward P. McGovern provided background information, as did former master Ottmar Friz and Capt. Wayne R. Berry, both of the Military Sea Transportation Service. Numerous Vietnam troop passengers and family members helped too, including Jerry Barker, Ed Christopher, Dean Wingrove, Leonard Kucera, Richard Plozay, Zeb Armstrong, Juanita Ingraham, Eugene L. Bechstein, and Rob Simpson.

In California, very special assistance was provided by Capt. Russell M. Nyborg of the San Francisco Bar Pilots and Jack Going of Baydelta Maritime. Barry D. Marsh, Winn B. Frank, and Frank O. Braynard shared information about troopship production, as well as the history of the *General Nelson M. Walker*.

We are most grateful to Carolyn Cox, for her assistance with transcriptions, and thank Gary Alter and Virgil "Wink" Casey for photographic support. Alletta Bell of Southern Cross Farm and her manager, Becky Hibbard, provided a much-needed transportation vehicle to move artifacts from the *Walker* to the museums. The Virginia Militaria Collectors' and Historians' Association, and members Greg Hosaflook, Ed Keller, and Joe Wayner, provided support and shipboard muscle.

Gerard C. Wertkin, of the American Folk Art Museum, offered his encouragement throughout the project and provided a very insightful "Foreword" for the book.

Ross Howell of Howell Press was again wonderful to work with, and his designer, Dara Powers Parker, used her creativity to create a first-rate work.

To my wife, Lee, I am most indebted for her patience, and her photography. She documented the canvases with great care, and artistically photographed almost every "nook and cranny" throughout the *Walker*, often in sweltering summer heat. Her editorial suggestions were invaluable.

Finally, our children, son Brent and daughter Laurel Cavalluzzo, contributed to the effort. Brent employed his research skills, joined in the search for veterans who served on the *Walker*, and was active in artifact retrieval work. Laurel also helped find ship personnel, and she and husband, Ken, graciously opened their home to us during research trips to the National Archives.

—Art Beltrone
Keswick, Virginia
November 2004

1 GHOST FLEET

The trip to the James River Reserve Fleet near Fort Eustis, Virginia, a place often called home for the "Ghost Fleet," had been arranged by motion picture production designer Jack Fisk, my Keswick, Virginia, neighbor.

Aware of my background in the study of military artifacts, Fisk had asked for research assistance in defining and locating the correct uniforms, equipment, and weapons for the movie *The Thin Red Line*. The film was about American Army troops fighting Japanese forces in the 1942 World War II battle for Guadalcanal.

The beginning of the film required the creation of a troopship set complete with crowded berthing compartment. In this area, the soldiers, played by actors Sean Penn, Adrien Brody, George Clooney, John Cusack, Woody Harrelson, and others, would be filmed "shooting the bull," shaving, reading letters from home, bumping into each other in the narrow bunk aisles, and struggling for an outside look through a very small porthole.

They would talk about home and the girls they had left behind, and speculate about the battle to come. The actors would offer a variety of emotions and sentiments. In the compartment there would be humor, homesickness, anticipation, and bravado.

To create the realistic set, Fisk needed to find the real thing. Research directed him to the James River Reserve Fleet and its aging, unwanted, and abandoned ships.

The fleet anchorage was established in 1946 to accommodate the hundreds of World War II ships that had come off operation. The James River facility was one of eight such anchorage sites established along the East, Gulf, and West Coasts, and at one time it alone contained more than 700 ships. The rows of vessels stretched so far downriver that in the most distant lines, only the ships' king posts, mast-heads, and topmasts were visible on the horizon.

When we visited the fleet on a chilly, February morning in 1997, it contained just over 100 ships broken down into small groups, arranged in separate rows. The rows are called "nests," and in the seventh nest, also known as "Unit Seven," was the *General Nelson M. Walker*. Fisk had learned that the troopship *Walker* dated to World War II, was still equipped with bunks in her berthing compartments, and was serviced with electricity for interior lighting and an operating dehumidification system. She seemed the right candidate for videotaping, and Department of Transportation officials arranged for us to visit.

Over the years I had seen countless newsreels showing American troops transported to war on big ships in crowded compartments. This was an opportunity to see firsthand just how congested the compartments were, and to relive to some small degree how troops felt within the vastness of such a vessel. The *Walker*, we were told, was 608 feet long—the length of two football fields plus room for cheerleaders in the end zone.

The information came from Fleet Superintendent Capt. Paul Smith and his assistant, Mike Bagley, who reviewed safety regulations and issued us each a portable lighting device and a large, five-pound, waist-worn battery that powered the lamp. By 8:00 A.M. we were joined by John Shaw, a fleet electrician, who would be our guide.

We boarded a small utility boat for our three-mile river trip to the *Walker*. Shaw was dressed more colorfully than the rest of us, with yellow coveralls over a navy-blue hooded parka. He also was equipped with warm gloves, heavy steel-tipped work boots, white hard hat, and, for safety, a brown-colored life vest. He too carried a small lantern with its large battery strapped to his waist.

Fisk and I wore warm clothing under our life vests, and on our feet, for added safety, had rough-soled boots for traction on the wet, slippery metal surfaces we were told to expect.

It took about thirty minutes to reach the *Walker*, because the utility vessel, with its raised, white-colored, flat, steel roof covering the passenger compartment, made several stops along the way. The fleet workmen, who sat below deck on thick wooden benches, disembarked periodically for work on various ship nests. Their job was to check mooring cables, anchor chains, and ship interiors. Some dehumidification systems had to

be monitored, and the steel hulls of the ships, many more than fifty years old, had to be inspected for leaks below the waterline. Tanks, still containing fuel, required inspection to prevent leakage of oil into the river.

The *Walker* and the rest of the ships in Unit Seven were fastened together in a standard fleet mooring pattern, each alongside the other, bows adjacent to sterns. The arrangement was maintained throughout the nest, which consisted of seventeen vessels.

Under a cloudless, brilliant blue sky, the pilot slowed the utility boat's two diesel engines and circled the nest of ships. We slowly passed the *Walker*, positioned fourth in from one end, and saw four large chains extending downward from her bow into the river. Two were on each side of the ship. Her name designation—"U.S.N.S. GEN. NELSON M. WALKER"—was barely visible through numerous layers of gray paint.

The bright sun reflected off the deck of our taxi vessel and glistened through the *Walker*'s tall masts and king post structures. Over the low, throaty noise of the diesels, Shaw described the nested vessels and offered some of their names— the *Santa Lucia*, *General William O. Darby*, *Vulcan*, *Canopus*, and *Santa Cruz*. The *Waccamaw*, *Canisteo*, *Truckee*, and *Cape Mendocino*. *Pawcatuck*, *Santa Isabel*, and *Henry Eckford*.

About fifty feet from the *Walker*'s bulbous-shaped stern, the pilot slowed our speed almost to idle. A large, irregular patch of rust sat just above the *Walker*'s waterline. In addition to the large anchor chains that extended into the river, heavy steel cables stretched from the ship's sides to each adjoining ship. The cables were not taut but were slightly loose, to compensate for lateral movement. Large wood fenders made of oak were positioned between the ships.

As our small boat moved past the *Walker*'s stern, we realized the rust we noticed was not a patch. It extended along the length of the *Walker*'s hull, toward the bow.

The utility boat pilot continued down the line and stopped the small boat near a floating wooden platform on the port side of the *Santa Lucia*, an end ship in Unit Seven. A steep metal ladder was affixed to the ship's side, which we ascended, camera gear in tow. Stanchions linked by chain and heavy rope were positioned along the ladder's waterside edge for safety. The steps were slick from the morning's dew, but the ribbed soles of our boots provided adequate traction.

With Shaw in the lead, we threaded our way through the *Santa Lucia*'s peeling and rusted metal deck structures. The *Darby* was dead ahead, identified by someone long ago who had used black paint to write the ship's name in crude letters on one section of its side.

A metal gangway, attached from the starboard edge of the *Santa Lucia* to the starboard side of the *Darby*, formed a short bridge between the ships, with small stairs positioned at each end, the bottom and top steps painted bright yellow as a warning.

The walkway was a sheet of rusted Marston matting, about ten feet in length. The metal, also known as "PSP" for "Pierced Steel Plating," was pierced with round holes and resembled a piece of Swiss cheese. It was originally used for aircraft landing surfaces on sandy terrain, especially on Pacific islands.

The gangway flexed, vibrated, and clanked forty feet above the river when we crossed. Below, the water depth was about thirty feet.

We crossed the *Darby*'s partially rotted wood deck through an unlighted corridor that extended from one side of the troopship to the other. It was like traveling through a dark tunnel, guided by the daylight entering from the opposite end.

Another metal gangway bridged the *Darby* and the adjacent ship, the *Vulcan*. The *Vulcan*'s deck was also made of long wood planks, but they were mostly protected by a steel roof covering. Despite this covering, the surface of the vessel's side seemed diseased, with large sections of paint drooping downward, like a partially peeled banana skin.

The *Walker* was now directly before us, but we still needed to climb one steep metal stairway aboard the *Vulcan*, using handrails wrapped with fabric and rope for a coarse gripping surface.

There was a relatively new aluminum gangway that bridged the *Vulcan* to the *Walker*, and before crossing, we paused to take in the *Walker*'s size and

state. Rust, in hues of red and dark brown, was everywhere. There was also a plague of peeling paint.

Time and weather had teamed to create on the deck before us, in almost a three-dimensional effect, a huge rusted surface that resembled the shape of the South American continent.

Metal lifeboats, inverted for storage and raised on sawhorse-like steel supports, had rusted sides, edges, and centerlines. There were lifeboats everywhere, in similar positions, and they combined to form a metal maze, difficult to navigate around or through.

The lifeboats were thirty-five feet long and just over twelve feet wide, and each could carry 135 persons. We had to stoop low to see their orange-painted interiors. Each had board seats, and passengers could move the craft through the water by employing a metal mechanism, incorporated into each boat. Wooden poles, which were nowhere in sight, were inserted into the mechanism, pushed forward, and pulled backward, to turn each boat's small propeller. There was a paint-encrusted manufacturer's plate on each boat with a March 19, 1945, date accompanied by "WELIN DAVIT & BOAT CORPORATION, PERTH AMBOY, N. J."

The farther we walked along the deck, the more deterioration we encountered. We passed small doorways with metal steps and railings leading to them, completely covered with rust where numerous layers of paint had peeled away. There was an abundance of peeling paint. The exposed metal surfaces of side walls resembled huge patchwork quilt sections, colorfully decorated in reds and browns.

One of the *Walker*'s two massive smokestacks, originally painted at its tip with two uniform bands of dark blue and yellow, the colors of the Military Sea Transportation Service, was terribly rusted. The dark brown rust patch near its top was rectangular in shape, and continued downward in lighter and diminishing stains, caused by the wash of rainwater. The vessel's other smokestack was similarly rusted.

Both smokestacks were especially ugly against the sky's vibrant blue color, broken by fleecy white clouds that had formed. Just below one stack and on an upper deck level rested more lifeboats, sides covered with reddish-brown rust and flaking gray paint. There were several lines of heavily rusted and disorganized anchor chain on the bow. Each chain link was about twelve-inches long, and covered with rust.

Shaw led us through a covered outside passageway along one side of the *Walker*, past dangling wires and two heavy benches, used by troops to sit, talk, or daydream. The overhang provided shade from the sun and shelter from rain. A cylindrically shaped exterior light fixture, complete with glass globe within a wire cage, rested near one bench.

Across from the bench was a metal and wood handrail. The metal had flaking paint; the wood's weathered and cracked surface bore traces of gray paint and crudely scratched initials, names, and hometowns.

"CANTON, OHIO" was barely visible, as well as "TERI", "SOL", "Jim", "VIP", and "TEP". A soldier from the west left his state's name in deeply carved block letters—"TEXAS".

Not far from the bench was a single door with a tarnished Yale padlock attached to a welded fitting that kept the door securely closed. Shaw took a key from his coverall pocket and opened the lock. He tugged on the heavy steel enclosure to make it budge. When it opened, the smell of stagnant air filled our nostrils. It was also the aroma of history.

ABOVE Traces of the past can be found everywhere, including exterior handrails with troop passenger initials and names carved deeply into the wood.

OPPOSITE, TOP Unit Seven of the James River Reserve Fleet contains the *Walker*, the fourth ship up from the bottom in this aerial photograph. (David M. Doody Photo)

OPPOSITE, BOTTOM "Ghost Fleet" ships rest quietly in the James River during an early morning visit. Summer heat causes temperatures to soar inside the ships, necessitating inspections and maintenance to start early each workday.

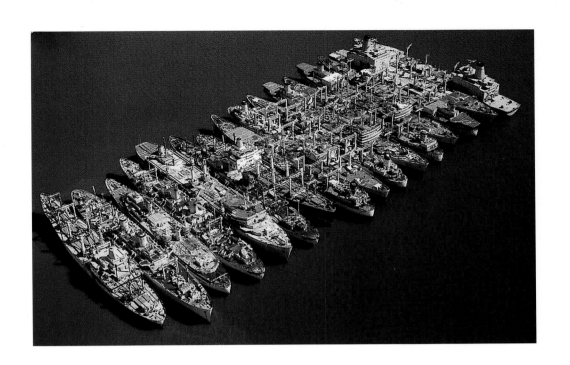

TOP LEFT The *Walker*'s massive size still exudes power, and the ship is double-anchored at its bow, deeply into the river bottom. Horizontal chains are fastened to adjoining ships for additional stability.

ABOVE The *Walker* is reached by first climbing about 30 steps of a steep metal ladder attached to the first ship in the row, the *Santa Lucia*. The ladder, with its flexible rope handrail, is viewed through the porthole of the small, utility "taxi" craft, used to deliver Maritime Administration maintenance personnel to ships throughout the fleet.

LEFT Rust covers much of the *Walker*'s stern, immediately above the waterline and below the ship's fantail. When the ship was in use, troop passengers would often gather in the covered area at the stern and watch the ship's wake as she crossed the Pacific or Atlantic Oceans.

TOP LEFT The *Walker*'s exterior is a contrast in colors caused by peeling paint and the formation of rust on the metal. Inside surfaces, however, such as the yellow-painted hatch (there are no "doors" on a ship), are often still vibrant in color, offering a startling contrast with the ship's deteriorated exterior.

ABOVE A rusted, open companionway, located on the *Walker*'s main deck, descends into a dark lower compartment.

LEFT A Military Sea Transportation Service (MSTS) poster found aboard the ship describes this closure as a "watertight door, dog-type." While still secure, it shows the ravages of time—flaking paint and rust discoloration.

14

ABOVE AND LEFT The *Walker*'s main deck is a metallic maze, with short ladders leading to small, raised storage lockers. Some of the ship's metal lifeboats, each bearing a 1945-dated manufacturer's nameplate, are stored upside down nearby.

OPPOSITE, TOP LEFT An open door reveals bags of salvaged Vietnam-era bunk linen, awaiting removal by museum personnel.

OPPOSITE, TOP RIGHT A light fixture, its globe contrasted against a wash of rust and chunks of peeling paint, no longer offers illumination. Protective paint that once covered the small glass porthole is mostly worn away.

OPPOSITE, BOTTOM LEFT The exterior doors of the ship are thick and heavy, and require an effort to open. The handles around the bulkhead are used to secure the door, preventing rain and seawater from gaining entrance.

OPPOSITE, BOTTOM RIGHT Steel rungs, mounted on flat surfaces, enable access to areas and fixtures above the deck.

TOP LEFT A pair of davits, used to suspend, lower, or raise a small boat, seem like sentries on the *Walker's* side. One of the ship's two smokestacks, traces of rust cascading down its surface, is seen against the morning's blue sky. The vessel's high "crow's nest" lookout station is at the left.

ABOVE A fixture that resembles a shower head and light are attached to the exterior surface, below the stanchions and accompanying safety chain of an upper level.

LEFT A ladder seems to extend from a covered, watertight locker, located within an alcove on the main deck. It instead is attached to the exterior bulkhead and leads to an upper level.

TOP LEFT An anchor is fastened to the ship's exterior surface with heavy, steel fittings above a rust-darkened section of deck.

ABOVE The many lifeboats aboard the *Walker* are made of metal, and they too display rust everywhere, even on the small, three-bladed propellers that powered the boat when turned by occupants using short poles attached to a mechanical device inside the craft.

LEFT The massive links of rusted anchor chain are wound for storage around one head of a "bitts" assembly, a pair of vertical structures used for securing mooring or tow lines.

2 MESSAGES

OPPOSITE

An open door permitted access to a lower troop compartment and graffiti-inscribed bunk canvases.

The *Walker* and similar vessels were built specifically as troopships during the latter part of World War II, and were considered to be among the biggest Maritime Commission vessels built during the conflict.

Two versions were created, an "Admiral" class (P2-SE2-R1), and a slightly larger "General" type (P2-S2-R2). The *Walker* was one of eight Admirals launched, and her original name was the *Admiral H. T. Mayo*. Her 608-foot length was supported by a 75.5-foot beam, her width at the extreme widest point. Her navigation draft, the depth she sank when afloat, measured about twenty-nine feet from the waterline to the lowest immersed part of her bottom. Eleven General-type ships, measuring 622.5 feet in length, were produced.

The Admirals were powered by turboelectric engines; the Generals had steam turbines. Both employed two propellers and had a speed ranging from nineteen knots for the Admirals, to almost twenty-one knots for the Generals. Troop capacity was just under 5,000 for the Admirals, and about 5,500 for the larger ships. In 1950 the *Mayo*'s name was changed to honor World War II U.S. Army Gen. Nelson M. Walker, who was killed in France during the invasion of Western Europe.

The *Walker* had six lower decks, numbered "1" through "6," and four upper levels, "01" through "04." As we cleared the door topside, our guide, Shaw, began to lead us on a tour of the vessel.

Deck 1, also called the "Main Deck," contained the purser's office, which was secured by jail-like steel bars. Here, too, were offices and state-room accommodations for key personnel—not just the purser, but the chaplain, chief steward, executive and commanding officers of the military department, and transient officers. There was also space for the ship's full-service medical facility, complete with operating room, sterilization room, dressing and treatment room, pharmacy lab, X-ray and dark rooms, dental office and medical officer's office, examination rooms, and small kitchen.

Troop berthing began on the second deck, with hundreds of bunks throughout a number of individual compartments. There was a large troop mess with colored chairs on the port side, and a large troop latrine at the bow. Fisk inserted a VHS tape into his video camera and returned with Shaw and myself to a small berthing compartment.

We could hear river water sloshing at the *Walker*'s side, not far from where we stood, video-taping rows of gray-colored steel poles holding aging canvas bunk inserts. The camera also recorded green-colored walls scarred by flaking paint, asbestos-covered overhead pipes, and the ceiling with its fluorescent lights.

The sleeping units we saw for the most part contained three or four vertically stacked canvas bunks, with the bottom canvas about a foot off the floor, and the top positioned with a bit more space from the ceiling. Most bunk frames were chained in at about a forty-five-degree angle, offering a clear view of the canvas undersides.

At one time the canvas berths must have been white in color. Now their coarse finish was tan from age, and many bunks were stained in a variety of colors. There were also some gray-colored canvas bunks, the color used on Navy ships. Some inserts had tears, and others had been repaired with strong thread. Each canvas bunk was just under two feet wide, and slightly more than five feet long.

Each multiple-bunk section, attached by vertical poles at the ceiling and floor, was also attached to the end of an identically tiered unit, followed by additional, similar sections. Attached directly to the back side of each row was yet another row of bunks. The multiple rows were positioned uniformly within the compartment, which measured roughly seventeen by twenty-four feet. It was very crowded.

Fisk walked slowly down the bunk row and continued to videotape. I followed with the camera case. Shaw stayed off to the side, out of camera range. When we reached the aisle opening, we were surprised to find drawings and inscriptions on one of the gray-colored canvases.

"1St BN. 27tH ARtY. HELLRAiSERS", the graffiti-inscribed canvas proclaimed. There was also the abbreviation "R.I.P.", for "rest in peace,"

next to a drawing of a tombstone with a cross. There was more graffiti, too, including a distorted skull, a tomahawk, a smoking Indian peace pipe, the state name "OKlAHOMA", and a soldier's name—"CHUCK WAllACE". There was a drawing of a cute rabbit with "C.W." and "OKlA." on its body, a foot with exaggerated toes, an ear, and two cartoon-like figures. One was a mouse, and the other a large-beaked bird. Messages left by a soldier named Wallace. But not from World War II, the period we had come here to research.

It was Vietnam War graffiti.

Fisk continued to videotape and paused at another decorated canvas, with its caricature of a grotesque head drawn with a broad felt-tip marker. The head, colored in brown ink, had a toothless smile and a few strands of wispy hair protruding from its skull.

"CAROL + THE COLONEL", the canvas boasted in oversized letters.

Another caricature, a humorous duck figure, was positioned to the side of the two names. We chuckled at the graffiti. "The Colonel" must have been a nickname. Down here, in this lower troop compartment, there would have been no one quartered with that high a rank.

We saw more marked canvas bunks spread throughout the berthing area. It looked as though a graffiti-creativity contest had been sponsored for the soldiers. A number were inscribed with the date 1967.

"Some of these are X-rated here," Fisk said, as we eyed sexually explicit drawings on several bunks. Other graffiti offered humorous, sentimental, or patriotic messages.

"THIRTEEN MONTHS of my LIFE gone BY, I'VE SEEN A LOT OF GOOD MEN DIE. I PROMISE THEY DIDN'T DIE IN VAIN, THEIR SWEETHEARTS will have A LOVER Just the SAME, ME!"

Large brass grommets lined the edges of each canvas insert. Once bright, the brass rings now had a dark patina. Some bunks had smaller, galvanized-metal repair grommets, and these too showed deterioration from oxidation. They had a whitish color to their surface. Sturdy rope was laced through each grommet and over and around the bunk's rectangular steel frame, strong enough to hold the canvas securely in place and support a man's weight and gear.

"CALIFORNIA GIRLS ARE OUT OF SIGHT!"

An adjacent canvas had a very unflattering cartoon figure of a female wearing a bikini, with large "FTA" letters—standing for "F_ _ k the Army"—on one enormously fat leg. Just about every canvas throughout the area, numbering in the dozens, had been marked with a name, message, or drawing. Some were crudely inscribed; others were drawn by more skilled soldier-artists on their way to Vietnam, or returning home.

"GEORGE WASHiNgTON SLEPT HERE!"

The graffiti-covered canvases provided a direct link to a past war, fought by American soldiers on foreign soil.

I had come to the right place at the right time. This chance discovery served as a catalyst for a salvage effort to preserve history, a project that ultimately would enhance the holdings of American military and history museums across the country.

ABOVE With video recording gear in hand and wearing a hard hat for safety, motion picture production designer Jack Fisk tapes a weathered section of the *Walker*'s main deck. This is the same area pictured on page 50, photographed in 1967 by a Vietnam-bound American soldier.

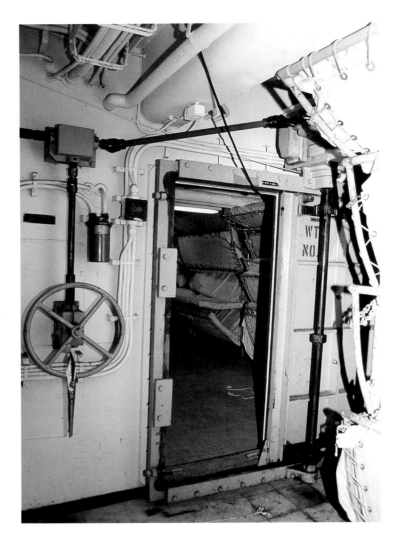

LEFT Troop compartments aboard the ship are separated by bulkheads, with openings to permit passage from one area to another. The openings could be closed by watertight doors, as described in a Military Sea Transportation Service (MSTS) poster. The placard identified this model as "Water-tight Door, horizontal sliding type." The large wheel at left was turned to close the door and seal off the compartments in case of flooding.

BELOW An unusually neat and clean *Walker* troop compartment is seen in a lower level. Most of the bunks are chained in a full-upward, stored position. At this location the ship's curved frames are visible.

ABOVE Bunks, still containing mattresses with covers, sheets, and pillows, were often stacked with orange-colored life vests. The orange color dates the life vests to the Vietnam era.

LEFT A graffiti-marked canvas bunk is laced to its frame and piled on other similar units in a troop compartment.

3 PRISONERS OF WAR

We had no idea the *Walker* was steeped in military history. I learned later through research that the veteran vessel had been in the national limelight.

She was built at the Bethlehem-Alameda Shipyard in Alameda, California, and commissioned as the *Admiral H. T. Mayo* on April 24, 1945. Each man in her crew of 400 Coast Guardsmen, with Capt. Roger C. Heimer in command, became a "plank owner," a term used to mark service as an original crew member. The end of the war in Europe was just days away.

One man, twenty-four-year-old Storekeeper First Class Earl W. Day, marveled at the ship's size. Her machinery plant alone cost five million dollars. Her engineering department, Day said, "was responsible for 20,000 horsepower, 80,000 gallons of fresh water every 24 hours, as well as 18,000 kilowatts of electricity." The fuel tanks, he added, could hold more than one million gallons of oil.

The ship had 106 vent systems, thirty miles of piping, more than 300,000 rivets, and 190 miles of welding. To feed a full load of troops, Day said, she needed 5,000 pounds of ham. One breakfast required 2,000 pounds of pork sausage and 14,760 fresh eggs. In addition, 7,000 pounds of potatoes, 2,500 pounds of sugar, 1,800 loaves of bread, 1,000 pounds of coffee, 2,000 pounds of pears, 800 pounds of rice, 540 pounds of butter, 350 gallons of ice cream, 1,000 pounds of powdered milk, and 12 pounds of pepper were needed to complete one day's menu.

By the time of her first voyage on May 24, 1945, American movie star Victor Mature, a Coast Guard chief boatswain's mate, joined the crew. The *Mayo* was ordered to Le Havre, a heavily damaged French seaport, where she would pick up thousands of former American prisoners of war and return them home.

After the troopship anchored a short distance from the dock, 5,819 anxious troops struggled to board under the weight of heavy, olive-drab-colored duffel bags, filled with clothing, gear, personal items, and souvenirs. They were entertained during the voyage by a band led by Coast Guardsman Warren Covington, a noted trombonist in civilian life. Tunes like "Swingin' on a Star," "This Love of Mine,"

"Oh What a Beautiful Morning," "Over the Rainbow," "It's Only a Paper Moon," and "Someone to Watch over Me" were troop favorites. Fourteen days later, after small fortunes were won and lost in card games, the ship and her passengers reached Boston.

Subsequent World War II voyages took the *Mayo* to Pacific Ocean ports, and she was headed for the gigantic Ulithi Atoll fleet anchorage with 5,000 more troops when the atomic bomb was dropped on Nagasaki. Almost two weeks after the war in the Pacific ended, her anchor was raised, and her course set for San Francisco.

She continued postwar service from West Coast ports, served Okinawa regularly, and became affectionately known as the "Okinawa Express." Then the *Mayo*, under the command of the Army Transport Service, was renamed the *General Nelson M. Walker*.

In early 1950 she was reacquired by the Navy, to be operated with her new name under the command of the recently formed Military Sea Transportation Service (MSTS). MSTS Master Ottmar Friz, with more than thirty years of seagoing experience, took command of the ship. Under his command, the *Walker* carried troops regularly to the war in Korea.

The veteran troopship became the subject of live, national television coverage when, on August 24, 1953, she slipped with great fanfare under San Francisco's fog-shrouded Golden Gate Bridge, carrying the first shipload of former American prisoners of war. The homecoming of the former POWs was big national news.

Newsreel cameras whirred as the San Francisco ferry boat *Yerba Buena*, her two stacks billowing black smoke, followed the *Walker* under the Golden Gate, a large "Welcome Home U.S. Army" banner attached to the upper deck of the bridge.

A fire boat, shadowing the *Walker* as the ship headed for a Fort Mason pier, celebrated the arrival by shooting streams of green-colored bay water high in the air. Bands on the *Yerba Buena* played "California Here I Come." A huge sign on the dock read "Welcome Home."

Former prisoner of war S.Sgt. Donald B. Disney of Ashland, Kentucky, captive in North Korea for thirty-three months, watched the festivities from the ship's promenade deck. He spotted a sign held high on the pier, and realized it must have been generated by his father, a Kentucky Moose Lodge member.

"S.F. Moose Lodge Welcomes Home Sgt. Donald B. Disney," the sign proclaimed.

"I couldn't believe my eyes," Disney said later. "It was such a thrill to be singled out."

A docking tug gently nudged the *Walker* toward her assigned pier, and almost as if by decree, the morning fog gave way to sun and blue sky.

Jubilation spread through the dockside crowd, and Elsie Norwood, a Port of Embarkation employee, began singing over the din in a loud voice. The crowd quieted and listened to her rendition of "My Hero" and "You Belong to Me."

First off the ship was Second Infantry Division PFC Roosevelt Lunn, of Baltimore, Maryland. Lunn, in a newly issued tan uniform with coveted combat infantryman badge over his left breast pocket, was met with a hearty handshake by Lt. Gen. Joseph Swing, the Sixth Army commander. Lunn's mother, and many of his nine brothers and sisters, watched the emotional homecoming on a television set in Baltimore.

A steady stream of 327 other former prisoners of war followed, cheered along by onlookers, until the last man stepped off the gangway.

RIGHT Ottmar Friz, a seasoned sea captain and *Walker* "master" during the Korean War, said the ship was his favorite, and affectionately referred to the vessel as "my baby." (Ottmar Friz Photo)

BELOW During World War II, the *Walker* had a different name—the *Admiral H. T. Mayo*. The transport, officially designated AP-125, is shown embarking American troops at Marseille, France. The smaller vessel to the right is French, sunk by the Germans, but still useful as a bridge over which the returning Americans cross to board the *Mayo*. (U.S. Coast Guard Photo)

LEFT The *Mayo's* first voyage, in May 1945, was to Le Havre, France, to pick up more than 5,000 Americans who had been held prisoner by the Germans. The men formed lines on the dock and waited patiently to board. The process took hours. (U.S. Coast Guard Photo)

BELOW Matinee idol Victor Mature, a chief boatswain's mate and member of the *Mayo's* World War II crew, is welcomed home by a group of Coast Guard Women's Reserve "SPARs." The organization's name reflected the first letter in each word of the Coast Guard motto, "Semper Paratus—Always Ready." (U.S. Coast Guard Photo)

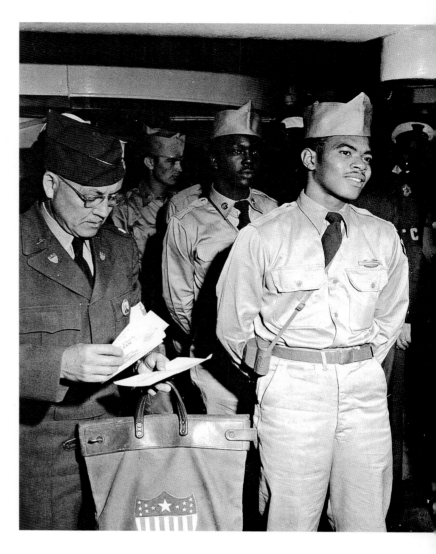

RIGHT PFC Roosevelt Lunn of Baltimore, Maryland, was the first former Korean War POW to walk off the *Walker* when she docked at Fort Mason in 1953. The smiling soldier wore a fresh uniform, adorned with a combat infantryman badge. (National Archives Photo)

BELOW American POWs, some held captive in North Korea for more than two years, crowded two *Walker* deck levels and searched the waiting crowd for family and friends, while an Army band played jubilant music. (National Archives Photo)

4 KILROY WAS HERE

After we had finished videotaping the first sleeping area, our guide, Shaw, led us into the other troop compartments, where we found more graffiti-covered canvas bunks.

It was not possible to move from the ship's bow to the stern in a direct line. We encountered solid bulkheads along the way, which forced us to take a nearby ladder (flight of steps) up, then down another farther on, to reenter the level we had been exploring. This was part of the ship's design, to prevent a large section from flooding if damaged during an attack. Large steel doors could be used to isolate incoming seawater within a smaller contained area.

I found the process to be very confusing, and somewhat alarming. I was afraid of becoming separated and lost, because most of the troop compartments looked very much the same. As we went up and came down, I would get turned around and not have any sense of direction. This was especially so in the lower compartments, where there were no portholes and you could not see outside. Often, when I thought I was moving toward the stern, in reality I was headed in the opposite direction. Fortunately, our guide was very familiar with the *Walker*'s interior and kept me on a correct heading.

Besides troop berthing areas, we found starboard-side rooms for transient officers, a troop office, day room, and small room that served as a store. There, troops and crew members could purchase a variety of items, including film, candy bars, and soft drinks. The shelves were empty, and a crushed paper cup lay discarded nearby.

There were also fan rooms and other enclosures to accommodate some of the ship's machinery, as well as a door that led to a freight elevator. Two large areas, called "machinery casings," were located near the center of the ship. They were separated by a large fan room and main stairwell. Each casing formed the upper part of the *Walker*'s two turbine-engine compartments.

The latrine area we visited was dismal. There were rows of white ceramic toilets with black seats and no covers, aligned in military formation. The inside of the bowls, ringed with stains, contained no water. Each toilet row was backed with an identical row, and there were several similar banks of toilets in the same area. The arrangement meant a seated soldier in one row would directly face another man in the opposite row. Separating each toilet was a round, open-faced aluminum bar, designed to offer a man support if the ship rolled in rough seas. There was also a long, open, galvanized-metal urinal trough attached to a nearby bulkhead.

Below the ship's waterline was the fourth deck, crowded with more than 2,000 troop bunks—the largest berthing area in the *Walker*.

"Get into A PIECE, Not into A WAR!", a nearby canvas advised.

Fisk stood in one corner of a large troop compartment, raised the camera to his eye, and videotaped the bunks.

"This shows you how the bunks are lined up to the side of the ship as it got wider," he said aloud, to record his comment for future reference. "We're standing aft."

The camera probed the compartment, recording more details. Fisk paused at graffiti on another canvas and taped the sentiments of a soldier who apparently was influenced by lyrics from the 1960s song, "Universal Soldier," by Buffy Sainte-Marie.

"YOU're THE ONE WHO MUST DECiDE WHO'S TO LiVE ANd WHO'S TO DiE. YOU'RE THE ONE WHO GiVES HiS Body AS A WeaPON OF THE WAR—ANd WitHOUT YOU All THiS KilliNg CAN'T GO ON".

The camera focused on a rusted section of bulkhead and two nearby, neatly stenciled admonitions—"NO SMOKING" and "CLEAR YOUR WEAPONS".

The bunks in an adjoining compartment were not angled upward, but were flat, as if awaiting the return of troop passengers.

"CAPITALISTIC YANKEE DOGS GO HOME".

Although the bunk rows showed order, the bunks themselves were in complete disarray. Each had a thin mattress inserted into a white cloth cover, one sheet, and a tiny pillow covered with an oversized pillowcase that seemed to be the size of a laundry bag. The bedclothes were stamped with a small "US" in black lettering to indicate government ownership. There was also a larger stamping—"USNS WALKER". The "USNS" was the abbreviation for "United States Naval Ship." The name "WALKER" designated the vessel to which the bedding had been assigned.

There were some blankets, too, but not many. They were olive drab in color and made of coarse wool. While a few blankets were folded neatly, the majority were haphazardly strewn about. Mattresses hung over the steel bunk frames at forty-five-degree angles. The pillows were irregularly placed. Only a few remained at the bunk's head, where they belonged.

"going to NAM JUNE 9, 1967 To SETTLE THiNGS DowN AND MAKE SURE CHARLiE IS TURNED UPSiDE DOWN."

Almost every bunk we saw, from floor to ceiling, contained a large padded life vest in no particular location. The Vietnam-period vests were bright orange in color and had loose, tan-colored fastening straps. They decorated the mattresses like spaghetti strands. There was also a smattering of early, 1950s-era, blue-colored vests, surplus from the Korean War.

"Give up the ship!"

The camera was turned toward a nearby wall and a framed placard. The small poster had four black-and-white photographs showing a female civilian and a sailor putting on a life vest. The notice also described the sounds of the "Fire & Emergency" and "Abandon Ship" signals, told when to participate in drills, and explained how to use the flotation vests.

Fisk continued to videotape other details.

"This shows the corner configuration of the bunks, how tight they were," he said for the microphone. "You can pretty well see the width of the ship. Probably forty, or fifty, feet."

Graffiti and drawings covered most of the bunks where we stood.

"Are you Afraid To die? IF SO, Well iTs BEST you go BACK home!!"

The camera was aimed toward a section of the ship that contained two rows of parallel bunks, with each row stacked four-high. All were in the lowered, ready-to-be-slept-in position, and the space between the rows was only about twelve inches wide.

"IN A FEW DAYS YOU'LL Be SLEEping HERE INSTEAD of ME. Wish you luck in Viet NAM. I MADE it. Dont know About you. you'll know in 13 Months thats if you'll [you're] still ALIVE."

A large yellow door with "ZONE 2" stenciled at its center was videotaped by the production designer. The steel door, designed to be watertight, was massive. It had a rounded top and bottom and six large, steel closure handles. The bottom of the door closed against a raised floor panel. We stepped over the obstacle to get through.

"ChArliE is going To gET you god-dam-it but I Am going To burn his ASS Too!!"

We were now in an adjacent troop compartment that had the same feeling of disarray as the previous one. A mattress dangled loosely over the side of one bunk frame, almost touching the compartment floor. Off to the left—in naval parlance, the ship's "port side" when looking forward (the right side looking forward is "starboard side")—the bunk area was darker than most, because a malfunctioning fluorescent ceiling fixture operated intermittently. In a two-second sequence, the light flashed on, then off, like a beating heart.

"VIEt NAM is No place for AN AMERICAN. But its A fight WE MUSt fight to KEEP OUR CouNty [country] ANd othER COUNtRiES fREE of comunism [Communism]. this is why you ANd I Both must fight. US MARINES Bound for Viet Nam January—'1967.' Herby Ellis."

Our hand-held lamps illuminated a darkened part of the compartment. There was a bright reflection from some rectangular object, located about four feet off the floor. The object was a small cork bulletin board, roughly two feet by three feet, framed on four sides by aluminum molding. It was the frame's metal finish that returned our light. The bulletin board had been the place to put your "mark."

Notices had obviously been posted on the cork surface. Numerous thumb tack marks were still visible, and one lone tack remained in the upper left corner, a snip of paper still attached.

Near the center was an imbedded staple. The board was inscribed, in marker ink, with the names and hometowns of war-bound Americans.

It was completely covered with first and last names, hometowns and states, and crudely outlined hearts containing the names of women.

"BROCKTON MASS" was displayed boldly in black lettering. "SEATTLE WASH" was represented along with "PACiFiCA CALiF.", "CLEVELAND, OHIO", "DENVER COLORADO", "TULSA, OKLA.", "B'Wood Texas", "JACKSON MiSSiSSiPPi", "Boone, N.C.", "SAVANNAH, GA", "SAN FRANCISCO, CALIFORNIA", "KAILUA, HAWAii", "AtLANtA", "NEW YORK", "NEW JERSEY", "IOWA", and "PENNSYLVANIA".

Two separate but touching hearts displayed the names "DEBBIE ANN WOODRING" and "HAROLD EDWARD FEIGLEY", while another heart proclaimed fidelity to "Charlotte Jo Adams".

Soldiers had noted who they were. We saw "S.C. Wells", "JIM RIDER", "RUGGLES", "ERNIE" from "BROOKLYN", and "TYrONE" from "DAYTON Ohio". There were "Mangini", "BOUDREAU", "K. MELCHER", and "SANCHEZ, J.L." also recorded on the board's surface.

There were places experienced—"FT. GORDON", "PLEIKU", and "VIETNAM".

A soldier had written his last name, "DuxbuRY", included his service number, and added "NEW YORK 67-68 NAM!!!"

And there were dates. "Jan 7 67", "6 OCT 67", "4 JUL 68", and "JUNE 1, 1966-JUNE 17, 1966", a reference, no doubt, to the number of days it had taken to get to war.

We stood, without speaking, in front of the board with all its names, silently thinking about what had become of the soldiers.

"I served my time in NAM
I've Really done well
So now I'm going home And
Really Raise Hell!!"

We continued our tour through the maze of troop compartments, using the narrower passageways between the bunk rows and the wider main aisles to explore more of the ship. Just ahead to the right, extending slightly from a bunk sheet, was a paper—*Stars and Stripes*, two-star, *Pacific Edition*, dated Thursday, April 6, 1967. Faded from age, it was a relevant relic.

"LBJ SIGNS $12.2 BIL. WAR BILL", the main headline screamed at the reader. Page six was filled with war news, some of it none too promising.

"VC Pound 11th Cav. Base Camp," the main story reported about the action ten miles south of Xuan Loc in Long Khanh Province. One American soldier was killed and nine others were wounded. "Helicopters fired on the enemy positions, routing the Communists," the story continued.

"N. Viet Downs 500th Plane," another story detailed. "The plane—an Air Force F-105—was shot down the day before the U.S. logged the highest number of missions over the north in five months. The pilot of the Thunderchief is missing."

The South Vietnamese also fared badly. One story told of a Viet Cong raid on a police station on the western edge of Saigon that killed five policemen, a policeman's wife, and three children. Another story reported a mine exploded in a military dependent camp north of Saigon, killing four and wounding eight civilians.

The sports pages offered a respite from the war news. Readers were informed that heavyweight boxing champion Cassius Clay (Muhammad Ali) would defend his title in a fight with Floyd Patterson at the Las Vegas Convention Hall. Another story said Yankee baseball star Mickey Mantle, moved from the outfield to first base in order to conserve his injury-ridden legs, "looks natural at the position, and he feels natural, too." The article added, "First base, even in the twilight of his career, was a necessity if Mickey wanted to keep on playing baseball (and making $100,000 a year)."

Just past this compartment, along a passageway, was a large cluttered room. The expanse had once been used as a recreation room by troop passengers, a place to sit and talk, play cards, or read.

It was also an area for church services.

Now it was filled with a jumble of orange-colored, painted metal objects of varying shapes and sizes, all resting on heavy oak pallets. The color was identical to that used on the life vests in the troop compartments. In addition, there were fire hoses, heavy steel cables covered with black grease, and boxes of unused bunk canvas.

The orange metal objects were for emergency use. There were small round canisters with screw tops, hard to open because of corroded threads. Inside were small, red-white-and-blue-labeled boxes of Diamond stick matches. The metal tops provided a watertight seal, keeping the matches dry and usable after more than thirty years.

There were small "Type SMC" signaling mirrors, still boxed in sets of two; lots of Type II, Mark 2 Sea Water Desalter Kits, dated 1967; small kerosene lanterns; and a quantity of cylindrical signal lights stenciled in black—"USNS GEN. N. M. WALKER". Each light had a watertight lens covering a bulb, and a length of yellow nylon rope attached around the body, which once held batteries. The desalter kits, lanterns, and lights were also painted bright orange.

There were orange-painted "USNS GEN. N. M. WALKER" metal fire buckets, too, and life rings just over two feet in diameter, with nylon rope attached around the perimeter in loops, to form handholds. The rings were also bright orange and stenciled, in large, black lettering—"U.S.N.S. GEN. NELSON M. WALKER".

They also had "SAN FRANCISCO" lettered on them, just below a multi-colored rectangular bar. Each of the bar's colored panels—black, gray, blue, and yellow—contained one of the letters that formed "MSTS," for Military Sea Transportation Service.

Mounted on a far wall, just visible beyond the large pile of metal emergency ration boxes, was a small, blue-colored wooden box, with the word "SUGGESTIONS" stenciled across its front in yellow.

The box was locked, and its rectangular top had a slit to receive suggestions. I used my light to illuminate the container's interior. A lone slip of paper rested near the box's opening. With the pressure from two pocket-knife blades I was able to retrieve the paper from the box.

It was a mysterious message, typewritten in upper case on an eight-inch by ten-and-a-half-inch page.

"NO MOVIES!!!!!!!" the message proclaimed. "WONDER WHY? ASK THE MAN WHO TORE INTO THE FILM LOCKER."

We encountered other messages as we toured the *Walker*, especially in the encased notice boards that were positioned throughout the ship's passageways. Most notices had 1966 and 1967 dates, but one, dated January 9, 1957, was located within a Plexiglas-covered case near another troop compartment.

It was the "Code of Conduct for Members of the Armed Forces of the United States," Executive Order 10631, authorized by The White House on August 17, 1955.

> Every member of the Armed Forces of the United States is expected to measure up to the standards embodied in this Code of Conduct while he is in combat or in captivity. To insure achievement of these standards, each member of the Armed Forces liable to capture shall be provided with specific training and instruction designed to better equip him to counter and withstand all enemy efforts against him, and shall be fully instructed as to the behavior and obligations expected of him during combat or captivity.

We continued our exploration of the deck's other sections, including its steering gear area, machine shop, engineers' workshop, electrical shop, and water treatment room. There was also a troop galley amidships with adjoining bakery, another troop recreation area, and, ominously at the bow, the "brig," or jail.

The brig could hold about sixty prisoners—troop passengers or crew members who had violated regulations. The overhead light was not working, so we used our battery-powered lights to illuminate the area. It had its own toilet and wash area, and the wall mirrors, instead of being glass, were highly polished aluminum sheets. Their sur-

face reflected images, but did not have the clarity of a standard mirror.

We continued down to the fifth level, the "platform" deck, where there was no troop or crew berthing. The ship's cargo holds extended to this level, as did the two engine compartments, separated by a cofferdam, a double oil-tight bulkhead designed to prevent oil leakage from one compartment into the other.

The area nearest the bow had a motor room; numerous supply storerooms for meat, fish, and milk; and several large areas for dry stores—food products not in need of refrigeration. There was also an ice cream preparation room with freezing chests, butcher shop, and thaw room. When the second-deck freight elevator opened at this level, meat and other food could be handily loaded and raised to an upper deck. The distilling plant was located amidships; its equipment converted salt water into fresh water.

Nearer the stern were more storage rooms for linen, ship's store merchandise, spare parts, paint, cleaning supplies, and countless other items needed to keep the ship operating smoothly. There were also two storerooms for the ship's stewards, the crew members responsible for catering to the domestic requirements of crew and passengers.

Deck Six was called the "hold," and contained space for dry cargo, boilers, refrigeration machinery, and large holding tanks for fresh water, fuel oil, and ballast. Ballast was the weight carried in a ship's double-bottom for stability. The hold also contained two motor rooms, the fruit and vegetable storerooms, and the *Walker*'s two propeller shaft alleys.

We finished our tour of the interior, and retraced our steps to explore the four, smaller upper levels—over the Main Deck.

Level "01" was the largest of the four, with offices and sleeping accommodations for the ship's officers. This was the *Walker*'s "high-rent" district. There were rooms for the first, second, third, and fourth officers; chief radio officer; chief engineer and assistants; assistant pursers; and deck officers. The ship officers' mess was here, complete with pantry and ice cream locker. There was a ship officers' day room not far from the gyroscope room.

Private toilets were in most rooms.

Beyond the "01" level was the "forward platform," used to store life floats, and beyond that, the "forecastle deck," with its powerful windlass that was used to haul in the anchor chain. Near the stern, on the same level, was the "docking bridge."

The higher "02" level contained two rooms that resembled a small penthouse. These were used by the ship's commanding officer. The stateroom had a large adjoining office, complete with conference table. Farther aft was the radio room, emergency generator room, battery room, cryptography room, and fan rooms.

The level also contained rooms for key ship personnel—the first and second radio officers, a boatswain and a carpenter, three masters at arms, two fire watchmen, and three quartermasters.

Above this, at the "03" level, was the navigating bridge. It was from here that the ship was run. The forward section, called the "wheel house," contained a binnacle, steering wheel, steering compass, engine-room telegraph, radio, and other equipment. A bank of rectangular, glass window panels faced the bow. They were now blackened,

to prevent strong sunlight from entering the command center.

Movement and engine speed orders were sent to the engine room with the telegraph, which had been removed sometime earlier. An elongated handle on the telegraph was moved forward and backward to signal various commands, including "Full Speed," "Slow," "Half Astern," and "Stop." Another telegraph, located in the engine room, received the orders. Loud bells rang to alert engine-room personnel that a change in speed or direction was being made. The bridge was the *Walker*'s brain. The engine room was her heart.

The opposite end of the navigating bridge, the area toward the stern, contained a chart room with large tables, fire control room, and radar room. The large cabinet drawers in the chart room contained nautical charts and manuals. Most related to the Pacific Ocean, from the West Coast to Southeast Asia. A twelve-inch signal searchlight was attached to the starboard and port sides of the bridge. Above the wheel house, at the uppermost "04" level, was the vent house.

There was no more to see.

RIGHT The bulletin boards aboard the *Walker* still contain official notices issued by the ship's master during the Vietnam era. This placard, directed at the civilian marine personnel who operated the ship, reviewed the "dos" and "don'ts" of their shipboard duties and activities. It was issued "By Order of the Master." It was printed in 1963 and used aboard the ship from late 1965 to December 1967.

OPPOSITE The front page of the April 6, 1967, *Stars and Stripes*, two-star, *Pacific Edition* found in a *Walker* bunk. The Vietnam War was bold, front-page news.

PACIFIC STARS AND STRIPES

10¢ DAILY   ★ ★ EDITION   15¢ WITH SUPPLEMENTS

AN AUTHORIZED PUBLICATION OF THE U.S. ARMED FORCES IN THE FAR EAST

Vol. 23, No. 95   Thursday, April 6, 1967

LBJ SIGNS $12.2 BIL. WAR BILL

Cruiser's Shells On the Way to N. Viet

A cloud of smoke and flames booms from the U.S. cruiser Canberra's 8-inch guns in the Gulf of Tonkin as it fires at Communist targets in North Vietnam. The targets were spotted by aerial reconnaissance. (USN Photo via AP Radio)

WASHINGTON (AP)—President Johnson signed into law Tuesday the supplemental appropriation bill providing $12.2 billion for the Vietnam war but complained about congressional amendments which curb the deactivation of Air Force Reserve and National Guard airlift units.

Johnson issued a statement in which he strongly urged Congress "to repeal these restrictions and to refrain from continuing other restrictions like these in the future."

He suggested this could be done when the legislators take up the regular defense appropriations bill.

The total contained in the supplementary money bill was $73.35 million less than Johnson had requested. The money is allotted (Continued on Back Page, Col. 2)

Chicago Re-elects Daley

CHICAGO (AP) — Chicago's Democratic Mayor Richard J. Daley apparently won easy re-election to his fourth term Tuesday with a better than 2-1 margin over Republican John L. Waner.

With 1,839 precincts of the city's 3,640 reported, Daley had 393,240 votes, Waner 146,337. Write-in candidate Dick Gregory, a Negro civil rights activist, had 4,436 and Lar Daly, another write-in campaigner, 320.

The Board of Election Commissioners estimated a light turnout of less than 61 per cent of the 1,722,610 registered voters.

Daley, 64, sometimes termed the last of the big city bosses, predicted he would win a fourth term by an overwhelming margin. Waner, 52, had declared his chances of victory depended upon (Continued on Back Page, Col. 5)

14 Accused Of Phony Deferments

NEW YORK (AP) — The FBI said Tuesday it had arrested 14 men who allegedly obtained draft deferments through the use of phony documents.

The arrests were made Tuesday morning after a Brooklyn federal grand jury returned indictments charging the men with violations of the Selective Service Act.

John E. Malone, assistant director of the FBI in charge of the New York office, said the deferments were obtained by mailing documents to local draft boards falsely reporting the registrants had enlisted in an armed forces Reserve unit.

Malone said the arrests were an outgrowth of an investigation of the activities of Paul George Miller and Solomon Gottfried, two central figures in a draft scheme that brought the arrest of 38 persons in March, 1966.

Miller and Gottfried h a v e (Continued on Back Page, Col. 1)

Speck Armed, Drinking on Day Of Murder, Witnesses Say

PEORIA, Ill. (AP)—A jury trying Richard Speck on charges of murdering e i g h t nurses heard testimony Tuesday that Speck had been drinking and had a gun and a knife shortly before the girls were strangled and stabbed.

Mrs. Michael Goze, who runs the Shipyard Inn in Chicago, testified that Speck drank in the morning, afternoon and evening of July 13 and left her place at 10 or 10:15 p.m.

The prosecution contends that Speck, armed with a revolver, broke into the townhouse dormitory of the nurses, about two miles from the inn on Chicago's South Side, at 11 p.m.

Patrick Walsh, a dark-haired, muscular construction worker, told the circuit court jury that Speck drew a gun in the Shipyard Inn in mid-evening.

Walsh said Speck sat in a booth just b e h i n d him. He looked around, he added, and Speck "kept staring" at him.

"I asked if I knew him from some job," Walsh related.

Walsh, who then had a cast on one leg because of a broken ankle, received no reply, he testified, and swung out of the booth.

"He (Speck) reached into his shirt and put something between his legs," the witness stated. "I seen it. It was a gun."

Walsh said Speck noticed that he had been injured and "put his gun back inside."

"Speck said, 'I'm sorry. I didn't realize your leg was broken.' He said, 'Sit down and let me buy you a beer.' So I sat down and started talking."

Mrs. Goze, who operates a combination tavern, restaurant and rooming house, testified Speck came in about 11 a.m. July 13, asked for a room and paid a week's rent, $10.

She related that he drank beer

in her place before noon. Later, while she was out on an errand, she said, she "saw Speck go into another saloon."

Speck returned to tavern about 8:30 p.m., she said, and ordered whisky and Coca Cola. He asked for a n o t h e r drink later; she added, and spilled some of it in the b o o t h where he sat with Walsh.

Mrs. Goze told the jurors she last saw Speck shortly after 10 p.m., and didn't see him again until she entered the witness box Tuesday in the Peoria County Courthouse.

Under questioning by Speck's defense counsel, Gerald W. Getty, she said she didn't look into Speck's room until police came to interview her July 14 or 15.

"What was the condition of the bed?" Getty asked.

"The bed was used—slept in," she replied.

She said she found an empty (Continued on Back Page, Col. 3)

7 Fires Raging In North Carolina

RALEIGH, N.C. (UPI) — At least seven forest fires continued to burn out of control in North Carolina Tuesday as the state marshaled its fire-fighting forces for a counterassault by land and air.

One person was burned to death and about 43,600 acres of woodlands burned Sunday and Monday.

37

ABOVE A cork bulletin board, originally used for notices, was found mounted on a troop compartment bulkhead. It was covered with signatures and hometown notations of the men who occupied the area on their voyage to Vietnam. The inscriptions were like initials carved into the trunk of a tree.

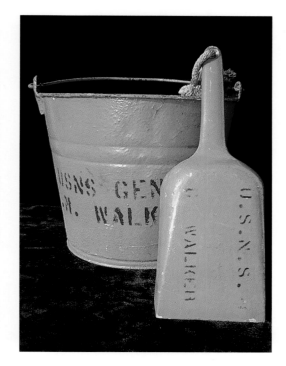

ABOVE A standard life ring found aboard the *Walker*. The letters "MSTS" stand for Military Sea Transportation Service and "San Francisco" refers to the port from which the ship operated.

TOP LEFT Historic artifacts found in various locations aboard the troopship include, from the left, a seawater desalter kit, an emergency battery-powered light used in conjunction with a life ring, and a watertight canister of stick matches. A photo on page 50 shows a similar light attached to a life ring that is mounted on an exterior main deck surface.

TOP RIGHT Almost everything is stenciled in black ink with the ship's name, including this bucket and metal scoop.

CENTER This stenciled wooden sign was placed on a main ladderwell bulkhead, separating "officer's country" accommodations from the enlisted soldiers' more crowded troop compartments. Enlisted personnel were not permitted to enter the officers' area.

TOP LEFT A section of one of the ship's galleys contains large round tubs that were used to steam food.

ABOVE A galley storeroom held china of varying sizes, decorated with a small blue anchor. The plate in the foreground was photographed as found.

LEFT The galley also contains a bank of ovens with stainless steel fronts that still sparkle.

BELOW Galley refrigeration units are positioned next to an open coffee urn.

TOP A "mess room," or eating area aboard the *Walker*, still contains rows of chairs in a rainbow of colors, neatly stacked on tables.

ABOVE The ship is equipped with a fully outfitted laundry.

LEFT The work room occupied by the ship's purser—the officer in charge of financial and other accounts—contains a small but heavy floor safe, its door wide open and contents long gone.

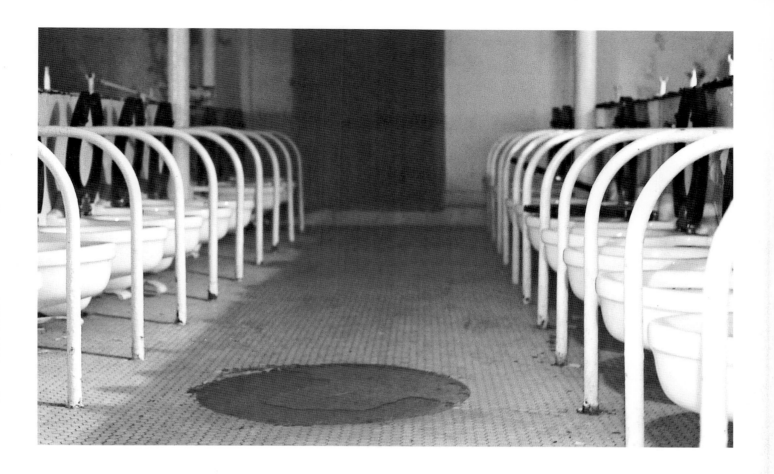

ABOVE There is no privacy in any of the ship's troop latrines. The toilets are separated only by metal handrails, available for use during rough seas.

LEFT Peeling paint is not limited only to the *Walker*'s exterior. Shower areas adjacent to latrines are equally affected. The small bags dangling from the water pipes contain the fittings used by the troops to turn the water on.

OPPOSITE Latrine-area sinks are made of stainless steel, and these lend almost a pristine look to an otherwise dreary section of the ship.

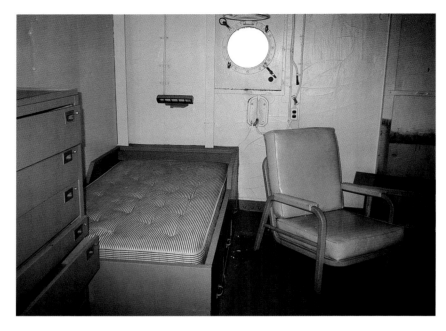

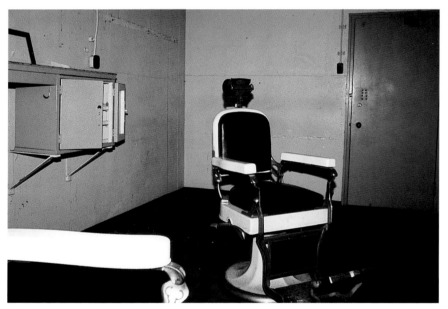

TOP LEFT The chaplain's storage cabinet still contains prayer books of all faiths. During voyages, the ship's U.S. Navy chaplain, as well as Army chaplains assigned to and accompanying the troop units being transported, were available to minister to an individual's spiritual needs.

ABOVE The Military Sea Transportation Service officers who operated the ship had more spacious and better-appointed accommodations. One officer had a platform bunk and much thicker mattress than the troops, plus built-in storage fixtures that could hold navigation charts.

CENTER The ship also contains a two-chair barber shop in a separate room. No remnants of hair clippings were found in the area; it had been swept clean.

LEFT During the Vietnam voyages, the troops carried their weapons aboard ship and usually attached them to the bunks where they slept. The rifles and pistols were to be unloaded, and stenciled signs were found everywhere on compartment bulkheads, reminding passengers of the safety regulation.

TOP The ship's bridge has been stripped of all equipment and serves now only as a storage area. The glass windows are covered with remnants of black paint, placed on the exterior when the ship was taken out of service, to prevent strong and damaging sunlight from entering the compartment.

ABOVE The *Walker*'s rudder control is long gone. Only direction signs remain, painted where the control was once located.

ABOVE Another "nest" of ships in the reserve fleet is seen from the bridge through one of its windows. This is the view the ship's master would have, looking forward, over the *Walker*'s bow.

5 MAKING WAVES

The *Walker*'s Vietnam artifacts, locked away for more than thirty years, were new to the ship in the mid-1960s, when the war in Vietnam sent a "wake-up" call to the transport at her lay-up in the Hudson River Reserve Fleet, just north of New York City, at Jones Point. She had been sent to the Maritime Administration facility after her last voyage, following the Korean War.

By 1965, as more American units were pledged to fight in Southeast Asia, almost twenty troopships were operating between Vietnam and Oakland, California, the major troop embarkation port. It has been estimated that the combined transport fleet force, which included the *Walker*, ultimately carried about 500,000 Americans to the war zone.

The *Walker* had been in the Hudson for almost a decade. She was partially stripped, and years on the water had encouraged deterioration. She desperately needed a facelift.

In 1965, U.S. Navy Lt. (jg) Harvey D. Johnston, a communications specialist, received word he was to be assigned as the ship's military representative. The *Walker* had been recalled for active service. Johnston was curious about his assignment and visited the ship at her river berth.

"There wasn't any power or anything on board," he recalled. "Going aboard a ship that's completely dead—no lights, no power, nothing—is a weird thing."

"It had been stripped pretty bare at that time," he remembered. "I looked around and I said to myself, 'Boy, it's going to take 'em awhile.' It was amazing what they were able to do in Baltimore."

At the Maryland port, the *Walker* was dry docked at the Bethlehem Steel Shipyard, and received her facelift at the hands of hundreds of yard employees, who worked around-the-clock shifts.

The naval officer became the first military representative to join the ship, and became the executive officer of its Military Department, which interacted between the ship's MSTS master and U.S. Army and Marine Corps troop commanders.

Johnston remembered shipyard employees being everywhere on the ship, getting berthing spaces ready to receive troop passengers, painting compartments, changing floor tiles, updating latrines. The metal bunk frames, still in place from earlier voyages, were scraped and repainted. There were no canvas bottoms, mattresses, or pillows. These had to be reordered.

Bob King, an MSTS steward department yeoman, participated in the facelift operation from a massive, three-story brick warehouse several blocks from the pier.

"When I first went on her I thought, 'What the hell are they doing with this thing?'" he remembered. "They should be scrapping it. It really looked bad. Especially when they had the red lead paint on her. And I thought, 'What a piece of crap.'"

King's job was to inventory incoming food preparation supplies—cups, plates, knives, forks, spoons, stainless steel pots, and everything else needed to prepare and serve the food for crew and troop passengers.

King also helped the deck department check in thousands of metal scouring sponges, absorbent powdered soap to clean vomit, kitchen and toilet scrub brushes, and a complete range of medical supplies for the ship's hospital.

Thousands of new canvas bunk inserts, mattresses, and pillows were shipped to the storage building, along with sheets, pillow cases, and blankets.

A diner, located opposite the yard's main gate, became a sanctuary for many of the workers and MSTS personnel, including King. There was no way to eat aboard the *Walker*, because asbestos fibers floated through the air, and hot welder's sparks bounced off steel structures. The sparks ignited flammable material and small fires often had to be extinguished.

By the fall of 1965, work aboard the *Walker* was finished, and the refurbished ship was ready for transport duty. She went to Norfolk, Virginia, loaded more stores, and set course for Charleston, South Carolina, to pick up her first Vietnam-bound troop passengers, members of the Army's 519th Military Intelligence Battalion. Among the men waiting in Charleston was 2d Lt. Edwin A. Christopher, who was excited about the imminent voyage.

"The long voyage would give me a taste of what our World War II GIs and sailors experienced," he explained, "and I was looking forward to 're-living' a bit of history." Christopher and his comrades were told, incorrectly, that the *Walker* had been a World War II "Liberty" ship.

The order was given to board, and Christopher and his comrades trudged up the gangway under the heavy weight of their duffel bags. Once the gear was stowed, the men returned topside to the deck rail and watched yard personnel release the ship's mooring lines.

"We wanted to catch our last glimpse of the USA," he remembered.

An Army band on the pier played a series of send-off tunes, including, as a finale, "Bill Bailey, Won't You Please Come Home?" Christopher turned to a buddy and quipped, "I wish that had been something different."

That was the start of the *Walker*'s Vietnam service. She served through December 1967, delivering thousands of American troops from Oakland, California, to Da Nang, Qui Nhon, and Vung Tau, Vietnam.

In that two-year period, American soldiers left part of themselves aboard the ship, on graffiti-inscribed bunk canvases. The scribblings served as testimonials, not only to their lives and the tumultuous era, but to their service to America.

They probably never expected their sentiments would be found years later, much less preserved.

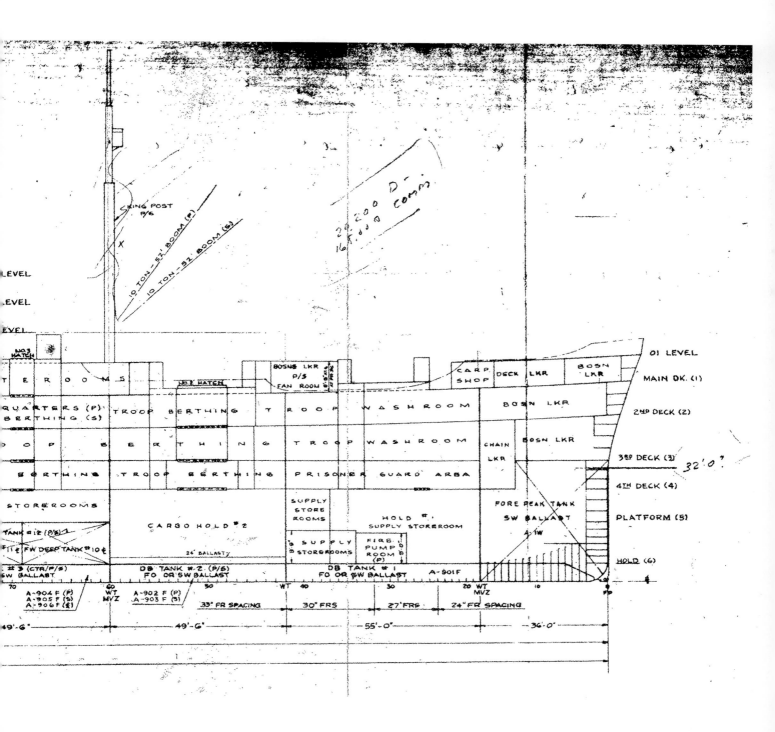

ABOVE Blueprints of the *Walker*, dating to the Korean War, were found aboard the ship. This side view, showing the ship's levels and compartments, was produced in 1951.

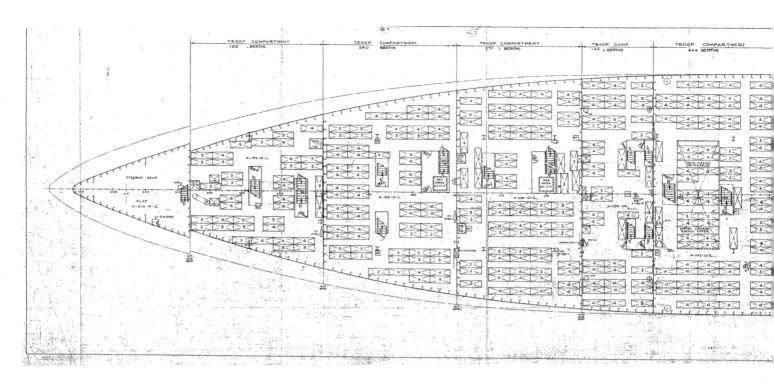

TIMELINE

November 26, 1944—P2-SE2-R1 troopship *Admiral H. T. Mayo* is launched at Alameda,
California.

May 24, 1945—*Mayo* begins voyage to Le Havre, France, to pick up and return more than 5,000
Released American Military Prisoners (RAMPs).

June 27, 1945–April 12, 1946—*Mayo* transports military personnel to ports in Far East, including
Okinawa, Tokyo, Manila, Inchon, Nagoya, and Yokohama.

May 26, 1946—*Mayo* is decommissioned from U.S. Navy and returned to Maritime Commission.

1946–1950—Under command of Army Transport Service, *Mayo*, renamed *General Nelson M.
Walker* (AP-125), carries troops from Seattle to Honolulu, Guam, Saipan, Okinawa,
Yokohama, Inchon, and Manila; then maintains regular triangle route—from San
Francisco, to Yokohama, Okinawa, and return.

March 1, 1950—U.S. Navy reacquires *Mayo* for operation under command of newly organized
Military Sea Transportation Service (MSTS).

March 27, 1950—*Walker* sails to Okinawa on maiden voyage as MSTS transport; during Korean
conflict, transports troops from West Coast to Far East.

THIS IS
The Ship I Sailed On

U. S. Naval Ship Gen. Nelson M. Walker

TOP This 32-page souvenir *Walker* voyage booklet was published in 1952, during the Korean War, and distributed to American troops transported by the vessel. It was produced by the Military Sea Transportation Service, was filled with pictures that showed life on the ship, and had a space on one page for the soldier to write a message home. It also included this untitled poem:

Men carrying duffel bags,
Bulging with
Close possessions,
Trod heavily up a gangplank
And then sail away.

It is with these men—
The men on foot,
The young men,
Where dwells the heart
Of America's strength
And security.

(Booklet courtesy Ottmar Friz)

Up the gangplank and leaving the States behind. The "big adventure" lies ahead.

CENTER The *Walker* voyage booklet shows American soldiers, duffel bags on their shoulders, ascending a gangplank onto the ship's main deck. The caption reads, "Up the gangplank and leaving the States behind. The 'big adventure' lies ahead."

BOTTOM Another photo in the Korean War voyage booklet shows bunks laden with clothing, life vests, and troop passengers. One man has suspended a photograph of a baby from a bunk pole fitting. The printed page caption quipped, "Not exactly the Waldorf, but at least a piece of the ship to call home."

Not exactly the Waldorf, but at least a piece of the ship to call home.

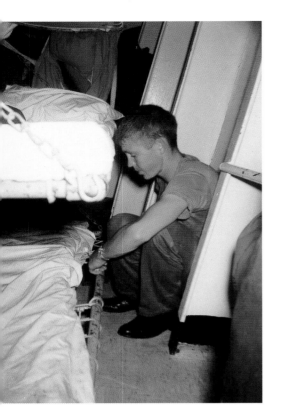

ABOVE A youthful American soldier, Vietnam-bound in August 1967, reties his bunk canvas to its metal rectangular frame in an area of the ship that had to have been very claustrophobic. The bunks were several decks down, crowded next to the vessel's side. (Eugene Bechstein Photo)

TOP RIGHT The *Walker* is tied up at an Okinawa dock during her August 1967 voyage from Oakland, California, to Da Nang, Vietnam. The reconditioned vessel made the stop to resupply and grant most of the troop passengers a brief period of shore leave. (Richard Plozay Photo)

CENTER The *Walker* is turned by two tugs at Charleston, South Carolina, prior to boarding her first, Vietnam-bound contingent of troops on November 12, 1965. Once turned, the vessel was gently nudged to the dock and the soldiers embarked. (Richard F. Halter Photo)

RIGHT U.S. Army 2d Lt. Dan McCarty caught up with his reading after the *Walker* left Charleston, South Carolina. The identity of the other soldier is not known. The bench on which McCarty reclined was videotaped in 1997 by Jack Fisk during preliminary set-design work for the movie *The Thin Red Line* (see photo on page 21). (Richard F. Halter Photo)

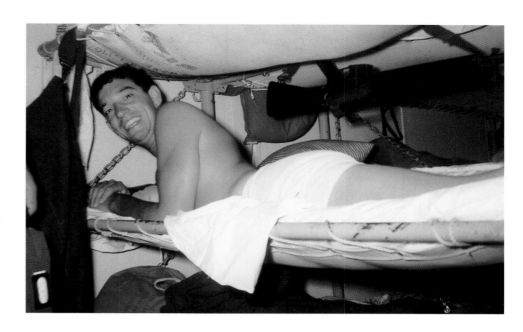

TOP An Army troop passenger in his undershorts smiles as his picture is taken by a buddy. His M-16 rifle is slung from the bunk frame above him. Graffiti has been placed on the canvas just above his head, and a "1967" date is visible. That canvas is depressed from the weight of its troop occupant. (Eugene Bechstein Photo)

CENTER Card playing became a favorite pastime in the troop compartments, and this young soldier seems to have a winning hand. The bottom bunk became an ideal seat, as was the deck and steel girder. Gambling with cards, however, was forbidden. An M-16 rifle is on the lower bunk to the left. (Eugene Bechstein Photo)

BOTTOM American Red Cross "doughnut dollies," a throwback to World War II, distributed cups of coffee to Vietnam-bound Army personnel before the men boarded the *Walker*. The photo was taken in 1966 at the Naval Supply Station, Oakland, California. Besides their issued gear, which was worn, the soldiers carried heavy duffel bags and M-16 rifles. (Naval Supply Station Photo)

6 SALVAGE

OPPOSITE
Artifacts from the
Walker were lowered
onto a James River
Reserve Fleet barge,
which was equipped
with a crane. Part of
the work vessel can
be seen below,
through the ship's
hawse-pipe with a
very rusted anchor
chain.

The sharp sound of metal pounding metal—like that of a blacksmith hitting a horseshoe with a heavy hammer—echoed through the *Walker* troop compartment, as two museum specialists muscled a sledge hammer in an unsuccessful attempt to loosen rusted bunk-pole threads from equally rusted floor sockets.

The poles were held in place at the ceiling with steel pins, and these were easily removed. But just below the floor level, the decaying metal pole threads were so corroded they just wouldn't budge.

The "clank, clank, clank" sound echoed again, followed by a loud "bang" from a steel crowbar that crashed to the deck. The sound, like that made by a small-caliber handgun, reverberated throughout the troop compartment and into adjoining berthing areas.

The sharp noise was followed by more pounding and audible "grunts," as curators and technicians strained against a steel rod that had been inserted into the looped chain that held one side of the bunk in place. The leverage against the makeshift fulcrum began to loosen the stanchion.

"We got two," an excited curator exclaimed from the adjacent compartment.

Two curators headed for a nearby section, but found the floor damp with moisture, caused by an apparent ceiling leak.

"There's too much rust there," they were advised by a technician. "Go to a dryer area where you've got a better shot at pulling them off."

Voices and pounding, not as loud as in our compartment, were heard from other areas of the *Walker*. Almost a dozen people, mostly museum personnel, were busy salvaging history on the dying ship. The *Walker* had been kept alive with the dehumidification system that served it almost as a life support system. The system had been turned off, and the ship was to be scrapped.

Since first visiting the *Walker* for *The Thin Red Line* movie project, I knew the graffiti-covered canvases, and other artifacts aboard the ship, must be preserved. They were part of America's military and social history.

Maritime Administration officials agreed, and authorized visits by U.S. military museum curators. The process was amazingly easy. One government agency simply transferred artifact ownership to another.

Over the next several years, during winter's cold and summer's swelter, my photographer wife, Lee, and I visited the *Walker* numerous times in search of relevant artifacts. We were assisted at times by our son, Brent, a Dickinson College double major in history and English.

We searched through the blankets and sheets of the rumpled bunks and discovered an assortment of objects discarded by troop passengers. The trash provided important clues into the ship's Vietnam-era history.

We found playing cards, comic books, a 1967 *Stars and Stripes* issue, empty candy bar wrappers, reading books, religious tracts, peanut shells, a single flip-flop shoe, empty cigarette packages, crushed drinking cups, and rosary beads. All were carefully collected and documented.

Larger historical artifacts were photographed and marked for potential removal. Curators at history museums throughout the country were notified about what was available. They responded with enthusiasm.

Dr. Charles H. Cureton, deputy chief curator of the United States Army and chief of Museums and Historical Property for the Center of Military History, was among the first to respond. He and his party of Army museum technicians from nearby Fort Monroe and Washington, D.C., joined us aboard the *Walker* on a warm June day in 2003. It was the second visit for Cureton, who had toured the *Walker* earlier, and concurred that her artifacts warranted preservation.

The U.S. Marine Corps Museum was represented, and Lee and I volunteered to retrieve artifacts for the Smithsonian's American History Museum, Department of the Navy's Naval Historical Center, Oakland Museum of California History, and U.S. Army Heritage and Education Center.

Most of the museums wanted artifacts, complete bunks, and graffiti-covered canvas inserts. Army officials, developing the National Museum of the U.S. Army at Fort Belvoir, wanted material to show how troops were transported by ships before the use of airplanes. The curators needed thirty-two complete bunks with clean, unmarked canvases, plus sixteen vertical stanchions, required to mount the bunks. They also wanted a large selection of graffiti-covered canvases.

Each bunk needed a pillow and pillowcase, sheet, mattress with cover, and canvas bottom. Thirty-two sets were needed, plus thirty-two bright orange life vests, one for every bunk.

The Marines received enough material to outfit a total of eight bunks, while the Smithsonian and Navy each received a complete three-bunk unit. California-inscribed canvas inserts went to the Oakland museum, for its "What's Going On?—California and the Vietnam Era" exhibit.

One California-related canvas featured psychedelic artwork over at least half its surface, and a large smiling sun. "Surf Club San Diego Calif.", read one accompanying slogan. Another proclaimed, "CALIFORNIA DREAMING".

The Marine Corps Museum received a number of canvas inserts featuring poetry and slogans. One was headlined in black ink, "Fight MAriNE Fight", and offered these sentiments: "WE ARE going INTO WAR. To Fight The Viet Cong. But NO MATTER whAT we have To do, it won't Take US Too Long. We will Fight & Fight untill we win This Lousy WAR And it will be the biggest mess that ANYONE ever saw!" Signed, cleverly, "By Gutson D. Deck".

Two canvases were of special interest to the U.S. Navy Museum. Both featured somewhat crude drawings of the *Walker*.

A large version of the ship, with an unfurled American flag at the stern and two smokestacks, was inscribed along its hull, "D TRp. 7th SqdN 17th AIR CAV. 15 Oct. 1967." The other canvas features a smaller version of the troopship surrounded by a series of slogans, including "WHY ME?", "HOW SAD I AM", and "DON'T WANT NO WAR."

The Smithsonian received one of the more unusual examples of graffiti found on the ship. The canvas was mostly inscribed in dots and dashes of Morse code, to spell out the soldier's name and address—"BOB SIMPSON 221 MARY ST PLAINWELL MICH". A communications specialist with an Army cavalry unit, Simpson also wrote mathematical equations on the same bunk.

The Army received about 100 inscribed canvas bunks, perhaps the only such collection in America, or anywhere else, for that matter. Every emotion and subject matter was represented.

There was humor in cartoon form. One soldier drew a civilian, who perhaps had just received his draft notice, about to jump from a hotel window.

"Room service?" the accompanying inscription read. "This is 1708…cancel that chicken salad on white…."

Another featured the politics of the era. Under a cartoon drawing of presidential hopeful Robert F. Kennedy's head, a soldier wrote, "FOR PRESIDENT RFK. RFK WON'T SUPPORT LBJ POLICY IN VIETNAM."

There were plenty of drawings of naked and semi-naked women, sketches of helicopters, tanks, rifles, and sentiments like that left by New England's Arthur Roussin, who dated his bunk "March 24, 1967." He wrote, "HEAdEd for ViEtNAM from So. Berwick, Maine. departed from Ft. Lee, Va, 10,000 Miles from home." He also included his home telephone number and "Ask for Artie, 'THE LOVER.'"

There were also macho and patriotic sayings covering the canvas bunk inserts.

"BONG The Cong", was on one; "I Killed THE KONg" and "KONg KILLER" on another. "I'm GUNG HO and I like it", wrote a committed soldier, and another recorded his service with "I'M A VEiT [Viet] VolunteeR!"

There were sentimental messages too, like that left by 337th Signal Company soldier Zeb Armstrong of Clover, South Carolina. The soldier had just married and inscribed his canvas with his wife's name—"BiLLie ARMStRONg"—and, "My dear Wife." He dated the insert "8/16/67" and added, "Viet NAM Bound. wiLL I Return???"

Music titles and partial song lyrics were represented, with inscriptions like "I'M SO LONESOME I COULD CRY", "Boots ARE Made for Walking", "TAKe these ChAiNS From my HeARt", "Baby I NEED YouR Loving", and "IT'S

Crying Time Again".

One soldier offered a prayer, written in red ink on his gray canvas bunk. He wrote, "NOW I LAY ME down to sleep, I PRAY tHe Lord my soul to KEEp. IF I die before I WAKE, I pray the Lord My soul to take. AMEN."

There were plenty of canvas bunk inserts with humor, recorded only in words.

"KILROY WAS HERE", one proclaimed. Another soldier offered, "KILROY WAS QUEER!"

"AT LEAST READING This gives You SOMEThing To do", wrote another soldier in 1967, and on June 10 of the same year, another man wrote on his bunk, "PLEASE HELP ME, IM BEING HELD AGAINST MY WILL!" The emphatic declaration, "I WAS HERE BUT I WISH I WASN't", was left by someone, and "Ho, Ho, Ho Chi Mhin [Mihn]!" was left by another serviceman.

One soldier's limited bunk space became the target for his sarcastic humor, and he wrote, in red ink, "THANK THE LORD for this SPACiOUS bunk", "PLEASE Obstane [Abstain] from kicking top bunk", "Shower DAiLY REMEMBER YOU ARE MAKING A LASTing IMPRESSiON ON Your bunk Buddy!", "TAKE your bunk buddy out TO LUNCH Soon!", and "No WRiTiNG Or KICKiNG IN THIS AREA".

A gentle Georgia soldier left a message proclaiming, "I LOVE TREES AND FLOWERS."

There were also references to drugs.

"BLOW Your Mind" was on one gray canvas, along with "legalize Pot", "Freak Out on Sugar", "CUBES FOREVER!", "LSD", and "Take Tea & See!!"

Some soldiers added insightful messages, like "…..BENEATH DID LIE THE GREATEST KNIGHT IN ALL OF GOD'S WONDROUS MORTAL NATURE…..SIR GERRY OF THE ROSE, AUG. 16, 1967."

Other messages were somewhat nonsensical.

"Hi THERE," a soldier started his lengthy message:

"HERE I SIT ON THE BIG WALKER. I DON'T FEEL TOO GOOD RIGHT NOW

CAUSE I JUST TOOK A SHOWER. I TRIED TO GET SICK LAST NIGHT CAUSE THERE WAS NOTHING ELSE TO DO, BUT I COULDN'T BECAUSE, IT WAS TOO ROUGH. THE WATER WAS NICE TODAY SO I JUST SAT OUTSIDE AND WAITED FOR A BIG WAVE TO SLAM UP AGAINST THE SHIP. AFTER THAT I QUIETLY CAME DOWNSTAIRS AND STUCK MY HEAD THROUGH THE DOOR, AND THATS WHY I WENT BACK UP ON THE DECK. MABY [MAYBE] THIS DOESN'T MAKE TOO MUCH SENCE [SENSE], BUT IF IT DON'T IT'S PROBABLY CAUSE I JUST GOT THROUGH WASHING MY HAIR."

He added at the end, "BACK WHEN US OLD SEA DOGS WERE LOOKED UP TO. FEB. 13, 1903. LITTLE SAM. FTA. U.S. ALL THE WAY."

The curators moved on to other areas of the *Walker*, after the rack poles and frames had been removed and staged in a passageway just below the main deck. We encountered a bulletin board, still posted with a notice from the ship's master. Dated "27 October 1966," it explained the comment, retrieved much earlier, from the recreation room suggestion box.

"The movie was restricted," the typed message explained, "by order of the Master because unauthorized persons entered a locked Navy Special Services locker through a loose side panel and removed films. The Master wishes to make it clear that if this practice should continue, the movie privilege will be permanently restricted."

The curators were taken to the small linen storeroom, filled with neatly folded pillowcases, sheets, mattress covers, white MSTS mess jackets and trousers, green surgical gowns, aprons, and tablecloths. Almost everything was stamped "USNS WALKER" in black ink.

The once-clean sheets, shelved more than thirty years ago, had a musty aroma. Nevertheless, enough pieces were bagged in mattress covers to outfit the museums' bunks. The needed pillows

and mattresses had already been removed from the troop compartments.

The curators were led down to the *Walker's* platform deck and into the supply storeroom. The big room was filled with an assortment of items, still in original shipping crates and packages. It was an artifact windfall.

There were brooms and toilet brushes, cans of cleaners, ceramic dishes, boxes of paper cups, syrup jars, salt and pepper shakers, cases of 1960s plastic spoons, and several rusted-out floor buffing machines. We also found nuts and bolts, rat traps, floor tiles, and empty buckets. The faces of the curators and technicians showed excitement.

Museum specialist James Speraw, of the U.S. Army Center of Military History, held a round cardboard container and smiled. He had found something so common, it was now uncommon, in his museum work. The container was filled with twelve bright metal cleaning sponges, made in 1966 by the Curled Wire Corporation.

"Very few people saved things like this," he explained. "Just your basic pot scrubbing pad. No soap on it. But it's a 1960s dated package. It's important. If I put together a display to show some guy working in a kitchen, scrubbing a pot, I now have something I can put in the background. It will have meaning to a lot of people who scrubbed pots and pans in the Army. Myself included."

Neil Abelsma, curator of Uniforms and Heraldry for the Marines, found other cleaning supplies in the same room. He made a pile of artifacts that included several scrub brushes, a floor broom, and cans of original 1960s cleaning solvents.

"I tend to look into the future," he said, after he added a can of vomit cleaner to his horde. "People don't save things today because they don't think the items are historically significant. A hundred years from now I'm sure they are going to be quite pleased at what we saved today. I retrieved items you usually don't see in museums, like the brooms, the handles, and the squeegees."

The storeroom treasures were staged on the landing of a main stairwell, and we further explored the ship. We examined a group of heavy, twenty-five-man, orange-colored life floats, stacked neatly on a boarded-over cargo hold opening. The floats were designed to hold emergency supplies in their netted centers. Troops were to await rescue in the water outside the float, wearing life jackets while holding on to short safety lines.

The thick oak boards covering the hold had small openings between them, and we saw light in the cavernous space below. The light illuminated the shapes of two large boats.

A long steel ladder, mounted close to the wall, was used to reach the vessels in the *Walker*'s extreme bottom.

The boats, each twenty-seven feet long, were equipped with engines, and each had a detached mast but no sail. These were the *Walker*'s motorized life boats, once kept accessible on the main deck. Although the boats were made in 1947, they were in excellent condition due to their dry storage, away from the weather. There was no rust, corrosion, or flaking paint.

The retrieval work complete, we moved the collection of artifacts to the *Walker*'s bow. The bucket of a crane, mounted on a barge, was used to lower the bunk poles, mattresses, life vests, and other items from the *Walker* to the work craft's deck. We also boarded the work boat.

We were exhausted, and found whatever comfort we could on black plastic garbage bags stuffed with soft mattresses, pillows, and life vests. Speraw, with the Army contingent, shared a personal emotion with another historian.

"It was almost spooky going through there," he said, between sips of water from a plastic container. "You know how many thousands of people have gone through before you. You are finding their fingerprints. Thousands of personalities are all intertwined into the whole body of the ship."

Abelsma, the Marine curator, offered his own reaction.

"Someone had been there," he said. "Just close your eyes for a second, and you can imagine the voices and what they are saying. They knew where they were going, but didn't know what awaited them. They must have spent a lot of time thinking of their past and future. I bet a lot of them probably said, 'If I get out of this, this is what I'm going to do with my life.' I hope a lot of them did make it. But we don't really know."

The *Walker*'s graffiti-covered canvas bunks, and a multitude of other historic artifacts, have become part of the Vietnam War legacy for future generations.

ABOVE A colorful greeting still painted on San Francisco's Pier 31 welcomed returning troops and ship crew members to the West Coast port. Vietnam-bound military personnel, however, may have noticed the artwork as well if they took one last look at the city's Coit Tower, standing more than 200 feet tall, a landmark on Telegraph Hill. According to some, the sign may date to World War II.

ABOVE During one visit to the *Walker*, time was spent searching through each individual bunk in hopes of finding traces of the previous troop passengers. Our effort was met with success, as we found everything from empty cigarette packs, candy bar wrappers, and peanut shells, to a headache and cold relief product box, discarded drinking cups, and a card game advertisement. A flip-flop shower shoe was also found under one bunk sheet.

TOP RIGHT The chaplain's storage cabinet contained a variety of religious tracts and books, including one song and service book that was published in World War II. A plastic Catholic rosary was found on the deck next to the cabinet, one portion of its crucifix broken.

CENTER A small number of liquor bottles and beer cans were also found aboard the *Walker*, under sheets or between mattresses and bunk canvas. The use of liquor or alcoholic beverages, by crew members or troop passengers while aboard the ship, was prohibited.

RIGHT A supply room in a lower *Walker* deck level surrendered a variety of shipboard artifacts, including plastic spoons used by the Vietnam-bound troop passengers and broom heads used by cleaning details.

FAR LEFT A small quantity of rat traps, in mint condition, was found in the supply room, ready for issue if needed.

LEFT A small glass pitcher was found, its interior surface caked with an orange-colored substance thought to be dried syrup.

CENTER Unused, Vietnam-era metal cleaning sponges, used to clean the pots and pans in the ship's galley, were found in cardboard, tube-shaped boxes.

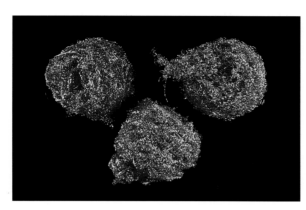

BOTTOM LEFT China plates were neatly stored in one supply room bin, and each had a sheet of protective paper separating one dish from another.

BELOW Plenty of unused cleaning supplies were found aboard the *Walker*, including brushes and scrapers, cans of scouring powder, and, perhaps one of the most necessary products used during any voyage, red-labeled cans of vomit cleaner and deodorizer.

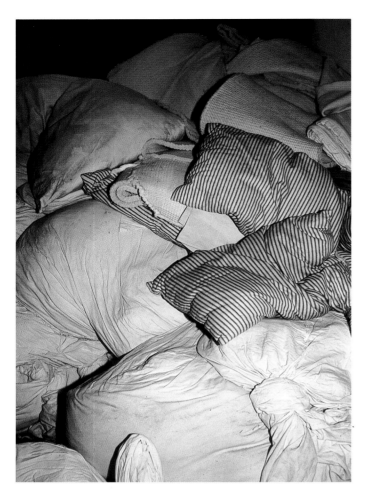

LEFT A pile of bunk pillows almost filled a small storage area within the ship's main supply room.

BOTTOM LEFT One area of the supply room deck was covered with unopened drums of "SOAP-TYPE-2" from "LEVER-BROS. CO. LOS. ANGELES, CALIF."

BELOW A storage bin holds rows of cardboard tubes, each package containing 500 paper baking cups.

BOTTOM RIGHT Another bin has unopened boxes of coffee filters; an unused, round thermometer; and a boxed lava grill stone from "GRILLMASTER."

RIGHT The *Walker*'s cargo holds are boarded over with thick oak planks for additional storage space. One area holds a stack of life floats, each designed to accommodate 60 persons in case the ship sank. When in the water, the troop passengers wearing flotation life vests would remain in the water and hold onto ropes attached to the float's outer perimeter. The inside of the float had a wood slat and rope bottom to hold life sustaining provisions and emergency equipment, including signal mirrors, battery-operated lights, and stick matches in waterproof containers.

ABOVE The ship's two motorized lifeboats are stored in a lower hold of the *Walker*, in pristine condition and still equipped with original motors. The boats probably were moved into the hold when the troopship was laid up in 1970. One of the boats is shown in the photograph on page 24, taken when the *Walker* arrived in California with the first boatload of former Korean War POWs.

RIGHT A life float is inspected by Army museum specialist James Speraw (left) and Dr. Charles H. Cureton, deputy chief curator, United States Army, and chief of Museums and Historical Property for the Center of Military History. One of the floats was transferred to the Army's collection of historic artifacts.

TOP LEFT Dr. Charles Cureton (left) and Art Beltrone sort bunk sheets in the *Walker*'s linen storeroom prior to their removal for museum use. Each of the sheets was stamped in black letters with the ship's name.

ABOVE Several museums wanted complete bunk assemblies with clean, graffiti-less canvas inserts. Removal of the specimens required several individuals working as a team in the crowded troop quarters.

LEFT A museum specialist carries a metal bunk stanchion up a steep "ladder" to an upper deck of the troopship.

LEFT A museum representative carries a bunk stanchion past a rusted World War II, 135-person lifeboat that was manufactured, according to an identification plate, in March 1945.

ABOVE LEFT Museum personnel moved a variety of artifacts to a bench like the one once occupied by Vietnam-bound U.S. Army 2d Lt. Dan McCarty for reading purposes in November 1965 (see photo on page 50). After all items reached this location, the objects were then carried to the *Walker*'s bow.

ABOVE RIGHT It took many hours of work to remove bunk stanchions for museum use, and the author, wearing hard hat and life vest, keeps his fingers crossed as the poles are lowered over the *Walker*'s side to a transport barge, waiting in the James River.

"Room service?
This is 1108.....
cancel that
chicken salad
on white......

OPPOSITE A troop passenger with a sense of humor and a talent for drawing placed this cartoon on the bunk canvas immediately above his.

ABOVE A soldier named "Bobby" drew a reclining, bikini-clad woman with Ho-Chi-Minh-style goatee. The graffiti was inscribed on the canvas during a *Walker* voyage to Vietnam in August 1967.

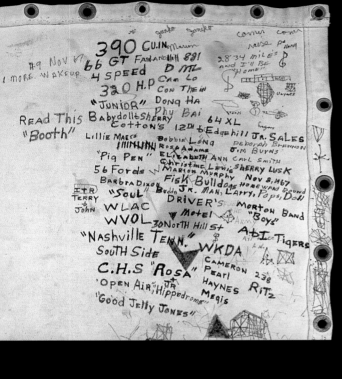

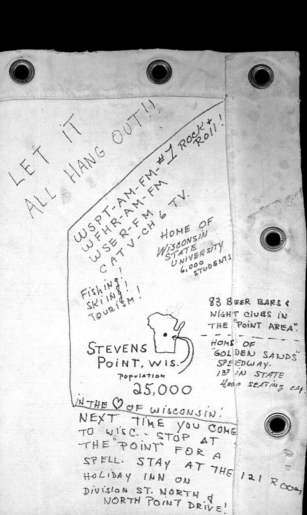
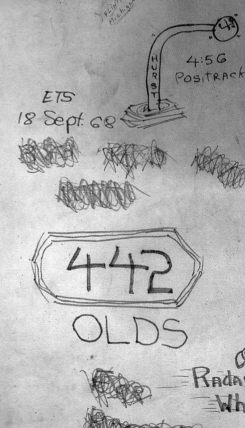

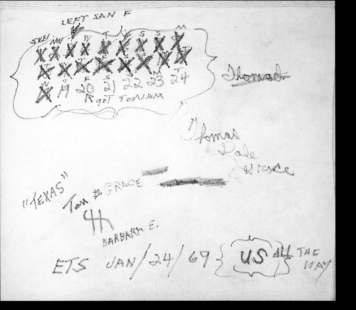

OPPOSITE, TOP LEFT Soldiers personalized canvas bunks with recollections of home, from radio station call letters to nicknames.

OPPOSITE, TOP RIGHT Some men drew renderings of military equipment and insignia on the coarse, canvas bunk inserts.

OPPOSITE, BOTTOM LEFT The names of hometowns, and places and things within those towns, were frequently placed on bunk canvases.

OPPOSITE, BOTTOM RIGHT The automobile was near and dear to the hearts of most Vietnam-bound soldiers. This soldier highlighted his favorite car.

TOP Graffiti in the form of a calendar was sometimes placed on a canvas to record each day of the voyage to Vietnam, which would take more than two weeks.

LEFT The soldier who placed this graffiti on a canvas bunk was a member of an armored cavalry unit. He drew an armored personnel carrier at the bottom and included the dates of the completed voyage to Vietnam.

BELOW A crude drawing shows an American soldier holding his M-16 rifle. The word "Kong" referred to the Viet Cong, the Vietnamese guerrilla fighters.

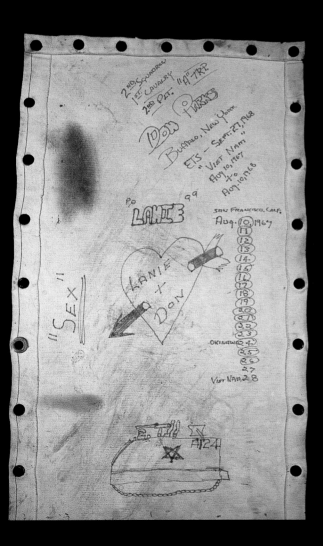

Encoded Canvas

As we entered the darkness and disarray of one of the abandoned troop compartments aboard the *Walker*, a canvas stood out like none of the others. Roughly half its surface was covered with Morse dots and dashes. A war-bound trooper had been creative.

The soldier was Army Specialist Four Robert N. Simpson, twenty-one, of Plainwell, Michigan, who had been drafted into the

service. He was trained as an Army radio operator with the 2nd Squadron, 1st Cavalry Regiment. He left his name and address with the internationally recognized symbols that stand for letters and numbers, along with mathematical equations relating to his military communications specialty.

Simpson, who earlier participated in theatrical school productions, also inscribed another canvas with Shakespeare's *Sonnet 29*, written out apparently as prose. Despite some misspelled and missing words, the soldier was able to record the work with black ink from memory. This canvas was identified by Simpson with his name using standard letters.

The soldier survived the war, but was killed in 1992 when the ultra-light plane he was flying crashed. Simpson's canvas is now part of the Smithsonian Institution's Armed Forces History Collection, National Museum of American History.

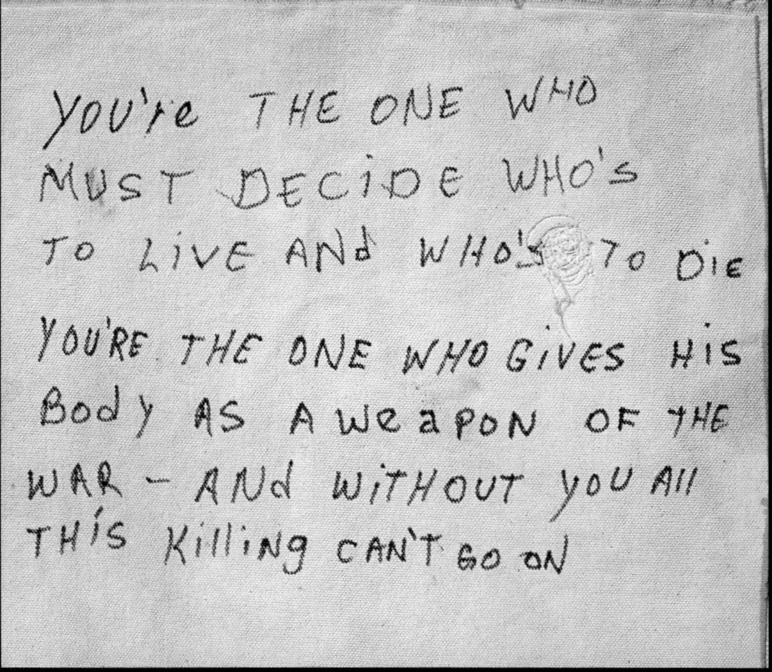

YOU'RE THE ONE WHO
MUST DECIDE WHO'S
TO LIVE AND WHO'S TO DIE
YOU'RE THE ONE WHO GIVES HIS
Body AS A weapon OF THE
WAR — ANd WITHOUT you All
THIS Killing CAN'T GO ON

LEFT This inscription was lef[t]
N. Simpson on the other en[d]
vas marked with Morse dot[s]
and mathematical equation[s]
the wording is not exact, th[e]
believed to be from the son[g]
Soldier," written by Buffy S[ainte-Marie]

BELOW Shakespeare's Sonn[et]
rewritten from memory on [can-]
vas by Army Specialist Fou[r]

WHEN IN DISGRACE WITH FORTONE
AND MENS EYES, I ALL ALONE BEWEEP
MY OUTCAST STATE, AND TROUBLE DEAF
HEAVEN WITH MY BOOTLESS CRIES
AND LOOK UPON MYSELF AND CURSE MY FATE
WISHING ME LIKE TO ONE MORE RICH
IN HOPE — FEATURED LIKE HIM —
LIKE HIM WITH FRIENDS POSSESED,
DESIREING THIS MANS ART AND
THAT MANS SCOPE, WITH WHAT I
MOST ENJOY CONENTED LEAST —, YET
IN THESE THOUGHTS MYSELF ALMOST
DESPISEING — HAPLY I THINK ON THEE —
AND THEN MY STATE, LIKE TO THE
LARK AT BREAK OF DAY ARISEING —
SINGS HYMS AT HEAVENS GATE —
AND THY SWEET LOVE REMEMBERED
SUCH WEALTH BRINGS, THAT THEN
I SCORN TO CHANGE MY STATE
WITH KINGS

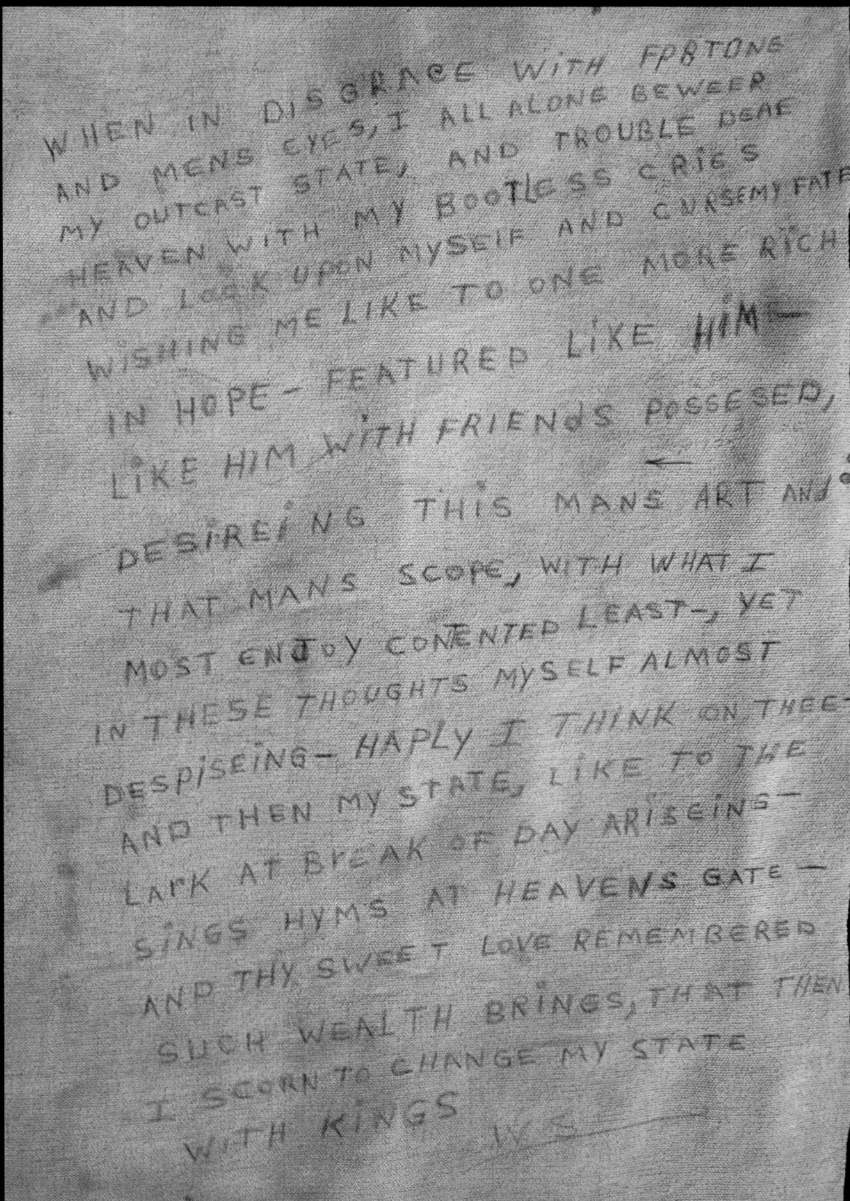

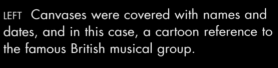

LEFT Canvases were covered with names and dates, and in this case, a cartoon reference to the famous British musical group.

BOTTOM LEFT A few drawings relating to liquor were found in the *Walker* troop compartments.

BELOW A Vietnam-bound soldier, most likely from a western state, created a somewhat psychedelic rendering, which he titled, "THE WEST."

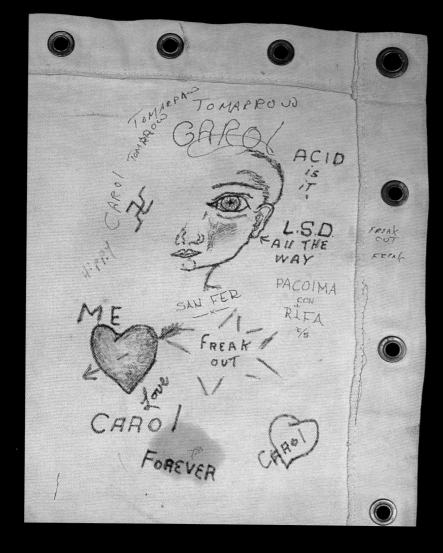

LEFT References to the use of drugs were sometimes included on canvases.

BELOW, LEFT AND RIGHT Women, clothed and unclothed, were favorite subjects for soldiers fantasizing about what they had left behind. Bouffant hairstyles of the 1960s are evident in the drawings.

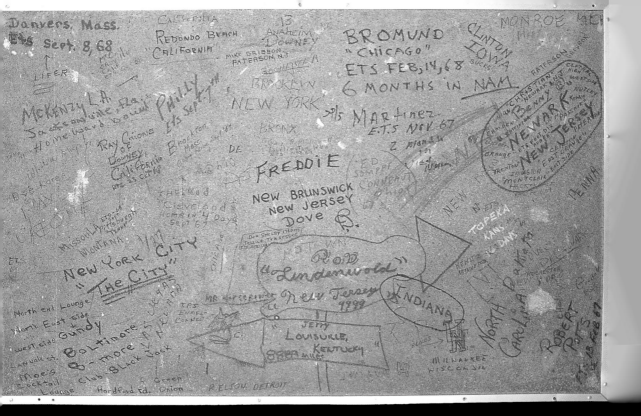

ABOVE Cork bulletin boards
… aboard the *Walker*
… re covered with all types
… graffiti, created by troops
… ng to Vietnam, mostly in
… 66 and 1967.

… HT The term "lifer" was
… ng for a career soldier,
… d "Lyle" was probably
… man's first name. Some-
… e put this none-too-opti-
… tic ditty on one canvas.

… RIGHT A soldier from
… tate New York neatly

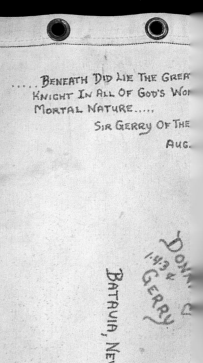

SADDLE UP, COWBOY!

Twenty-year-old Leonard Kucera used his thirty-nine-cent "Draws-a-Lot" marker to inscribe on the canvas above him, "Worlds FuTuRE 'bAREbAcK bRONC RiDiNg CHAMPION." It was his personal dream.

Instead, he became a trooper and mechanic with a cavalry regiment, bound for Vietnam in August 1967. A year earlier he had driven a 1964 Chevrolet Biscayne to rodeos throughout his native state of Nebraska, as well as South Dakota, Iowa, and Colorado. His specialty was riding bareback on bucking horses like "Redigo" (see photo below).

"I made all the rodeos I could in the region," he recalled later. There was little financial reward, but plenty of enjoyment. "I guess I barely made enough to keep going." He loved what he was doing. Then, in late fall 1966, he was drafted into the Army. It was a hard transition.

"I felt like I should serve," he explained, "but I also felt like I was giving up two of the best years of my life, because of my life in rodeo."

After the war, the 1st Squadron, 1st Cavalry Regiment veteran reentered rodeos, was injured, and ended his bareback riding career. He became a research technician at the U.S. Meat Animal Research Center, Clay Center, Nebraska.

The onetime cowboy displayed his graffiti-inscribed canvas to Army buddies during a 1998 squadron reunion. The canvas is in the Collection of the National Museum of the United States Army, Center of Military History, Washington, D.C.

LEFT AND OPPOSITE, BOTTOM A complete bunk canvas was used by one soldier to incorporate the popular Charlie Brown comic strip character into the combat environment of Vietnam. At the end of the panel the original Charlie is crying for help from a heated caldron.

BOTTOM LEFT Two American soldiers are shown escorting an enemy soldier on this canvas, which was repaired with heavy stitching, evident just to the right of the figure in the foreground.

BELOW, TOP AND BOTTOM Many of the canvases had small statements with big meanings. The "Ho, Ho…" canvas poked fun at Ho Chi Minh, leader of the Vietnamese revolution. "Bong The Cong" was another soldier's way to encourage his comrades to defeat the enemy.

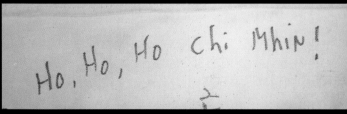

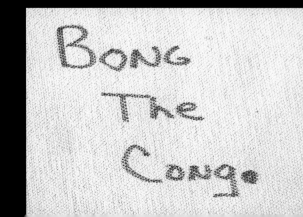

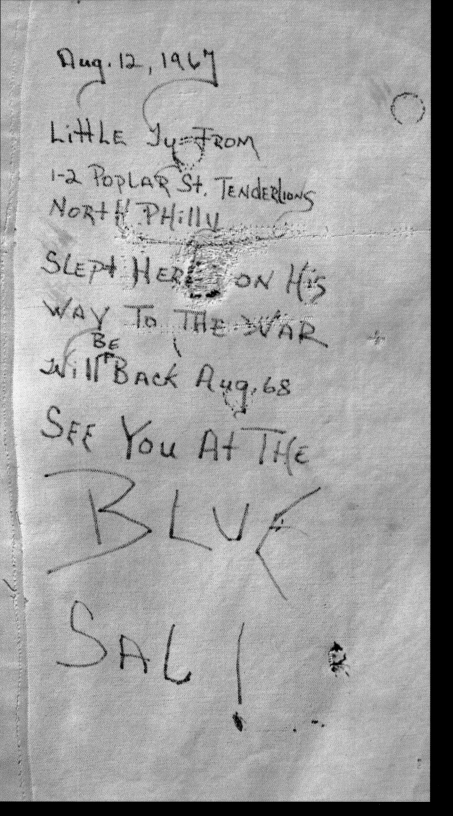

Aug. 12, 1967

Little Ty From
1-2 Poplar St. Tenderlions
North Philly

Slept Here on His
Way To The War.
Be
Will Back Aug. 68

See You At The

BLUE

SAL!

Nor What It Seems

The canvas appealed to us with its optimism—"Will be back Aug. 68. See you at the Blue Sal!"

The soldier, identified only as "Little Ty from 1-2 Poplar St. Tenderlions North Philly," inscribed the graffiti on August 12, 1967. He noted he had "Slept Here on His Way to the War."

An effort was made to find Little Ty, but the address doesn't exist. The *Philadelphia Inquirer* even ran a feature story, on June 27, 2004, headlined "On a ship to Vietnam, the mystery of 'Little Ty,'" but he did not come forward, nor did anyone who knew him.

A longtime Philadelphia resident helped decipher the graffiti's real meaning. The address "1-2 Poplar Street," according to John P. Buchanan, a detective in the Philadelphia District Attorney's office, was actually the corner of 12th and Poplar Streets, a dangerous 1960s gang location.

"Tenderlions" was pronounced "Tender-Lines," and was the name of an area gang, the detective explained. The "Blue Sal" could have been a bar or a candy store painted blue. "The 'Blue Sal,'" Buchanan said, "was most likely a location where Little Ty would 'hang.'"

"Little Ty's" canvas is now part of the Smithsonian Institution's Armed Forces History Collection, National Museum of American History.

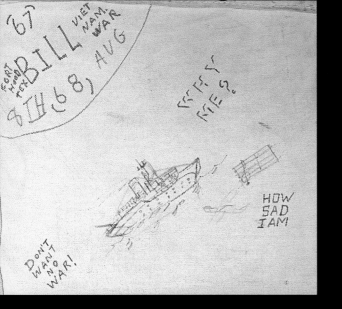

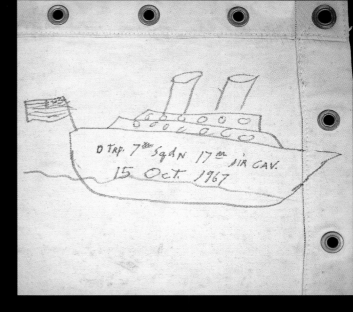

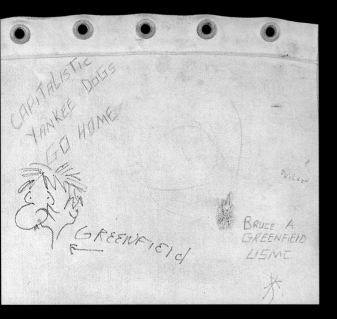

TOP LEFT Sailing on the *Walker* had a profound effect on one man, and he drew his interpretation of the ship on a canvas along with two forlorn messages and the proclamation, "DON'T WANT NO WAR!"

TOP RIGHT Another version of the troopship was hastily drawn by an air cavalry member, who decorated the ship's hull with his unit designation.

ABOVE A *Walker* troop passenger most likely assigned to a helicopter unit left his version of what seems to be a CH-46 transport, along with his name, "AL," and the notation "SHORT." The term was used to indicate his military service was almost over.

LEFT A U.S. Marine bound for Vietnam left a caricature and political message on his canvas.

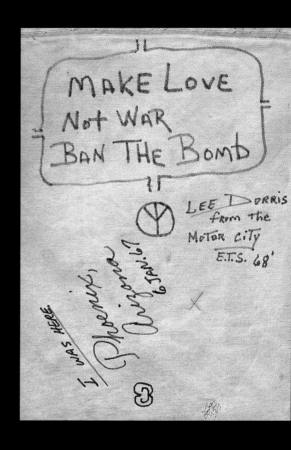

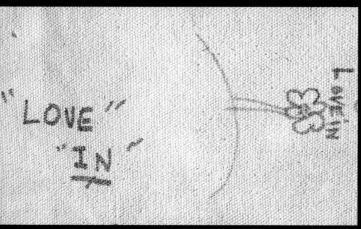

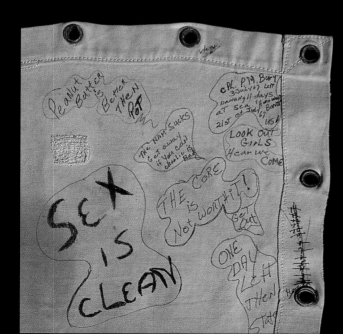

TOP LEFT It was unusual to find a color, other than black, on a graffiti-covered canvas. "Dave" used green ink to note the love he and "Jeslyn" shared.

ABOVE A favorite slogan of the 1960s and a peace symbol were inscribed on a canvas by "Lee Dorris," from Detroit, Michigan's "Motor City."

CENTER LEFT A practice of the 1960s counter-culture movement was the target of this inscribed comment.

LEFT One troop passenger inscribed his comments about a variety of subjects—including sex.

"Give up the s[...]

AT LEAST READING
This gives you something
To do.

1967

TJC
ETS

PLESE
HELP
ME, IM
BEING HELD
AGAINST MY
WILL!
E.T.S.
JUNE 10, 1967

JULY 26, 1968

TOP LEFT A soldier with a sense of humor inscribed the George Washington notation [and] added the 1789 date as the Revolutionary commander's E.T.S., or "Estimated Time of Separation" from service. The Mickey Mou[se] ears and word "ARMY" with pointed arrow[s sug]gest the soldier's attitude toward rules and [red] tape.

TOP RIGHT The most popular piece of graffiti [of] all time was this slogan. The wording has i[ts] roots in World War II, when it seemed to b[e] written everywhere.

ABOVE Along the edge of a canvas, someon[e] wrote his own version of United States Navy [captain] James Lawrence's immortal War of 1812 dy[ing] declaration aboard his defeated Chesapeake[:] "Don't give up the ship, blow her up."

CENTER LEFT Someone gave a reason for pl[acing] graffiti on bunk canvases. In a sense, it wa[s] graffiti about graffiti.

LEFT A man who was probably drafted into [the] Army added a 1967 plea to a bunk canva[s. He] expected to be released from service in Jul[y of] the following year.

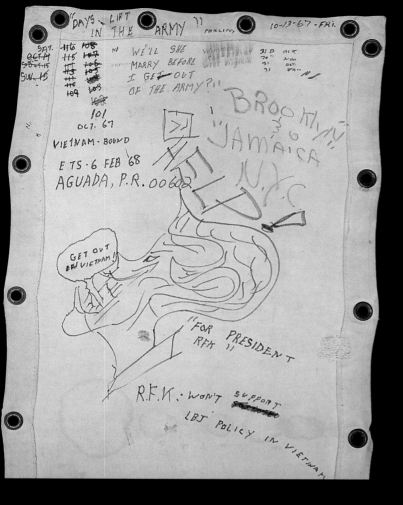

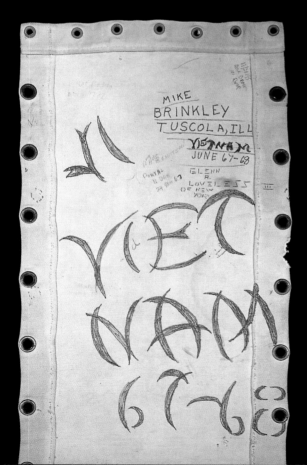

TOP LEFT The politics of the Vietnam era became the graffiti subject for this soldier, who wanted Robert F. Kennedy to be president of the United States.

ABOVE One of the first graffiti-covered canvases spotted aboard the *Walker* contained an assortment of images and the name "Chuck Wallace" and his home state, "Oklahoma." A small number of blue-gray canvases like this one were found throughout the ship.

LEFT The lettering on this canvas showed a Southeast Asian influence. The soldier noted his service year was from 1967 to 1968.

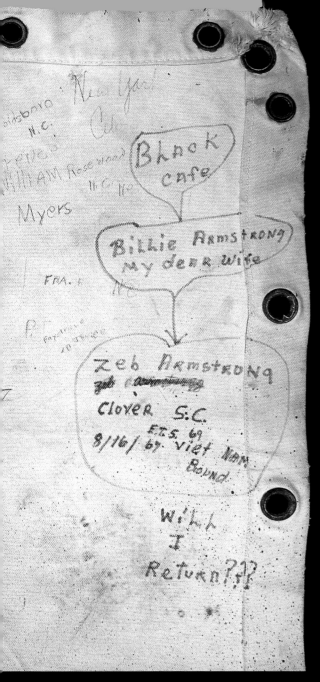

He Did Return

In the fall of 1966, Zeb Armstrong of Clover, South Carolina, was nineteen, making about seventy-five dollars a week at a textile mill, and newly married to wife "Billie." The couple had rented a house and ordered furniture.

By the following January, the mill worker was wearing military fatigues as he trained to repair radios as a member of the 337th Signal Company. In August 1967, he was aboard the troopship *Walker* headed for Vietnam.

Deeply in love, he inscribed a bunk canvas with his wife's name, "Billie Armstrong," then added, "My Dear Wife." He also wrote "Black Cafe [Café]," the name of a local hangout, owned and operated by Mabel Black, where he, Billie, and other teenagers met, ate hot dogs or hamburgers, and danced to the juke box.

When in groups aboard the ship, there was never talk about fear of what was to come. Troops kept such thoughts to themselves, or maybe shared them with a "buddy." In a quiet moment, Armstrong used a marker to write, "Will I Return???"

Asked almost forty years later if he remembered being scared during the voyage, he responded, "Going over there? Oh, yeah."

In the photo above, Armstrong stands with his wife, Billie, in January 2004, at the former Black Café in Clover, South Carolina. His canvas is in the Collection of the National Museum of the

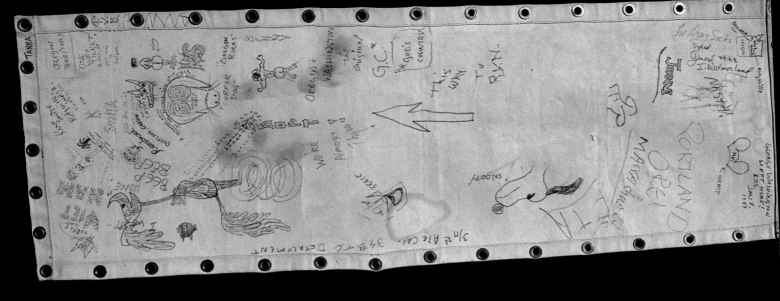

THIS PAGE AND OPPOSITE An abundance of graffiti was placed on this bunk canvas, in several colors. To occupy his time and ward off boredom, the soldier inscribed everything from cartoon characters, including "Surfer Dog," to names of places, and a voyage calendar with the comment, "We're Almost There!" Other men in the troop compartment may have added to the canvas.

OPPOSITE, BOTTOM Smithsonian Institution museum specialist Kathleen Golden and author Art Beltrone inspect the "Surfer Dog" canvas that was selected for the Armed Forces History Collection at the National Museum of American History.

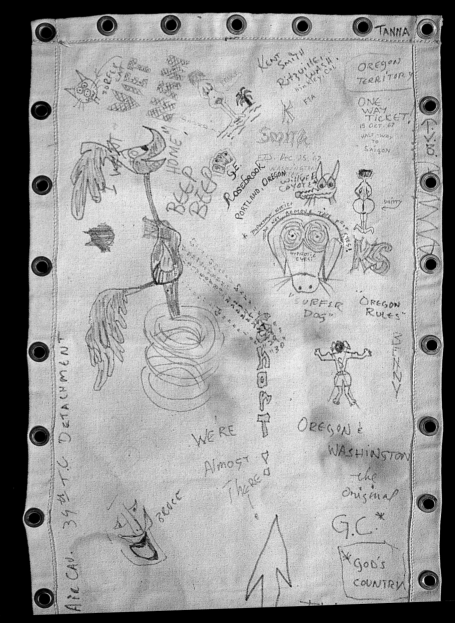

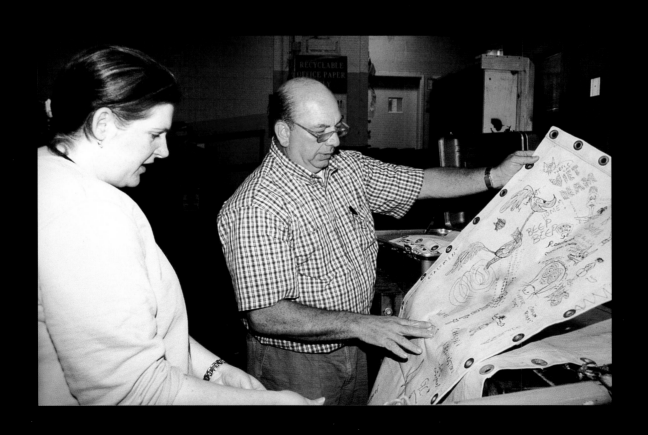

THE PERFECT SPOT

On a hot July morning in 1998, Jerry Barker leaned on the *Walker*'s stern railing and stared at the James River. He was shielded from the sun by the steel overhead of the ship's main deck. Large steel vertical girders around the stern created gigantic "picture windows" in this "room."

In 1967, Barker, then twenty, and his 2nd Squadron, 1st Cavalry comrades, were on a crowded *Walker* going to war. "It was full of people," he remembered, "always people, wherever you went."

Before long Barker found personal space at the ship's stern. "At night there was nothing neater than the dark with a zillion stars," he recalled. "And you'd hear a 'swrrrrr' sound, going through the water. It was one of those places you could get away to and be by yourself. This was the perfect spot."

He paused on the *Walker*'s main deck at the end of his visit to the rusting ship, lost in his thoughts.

"She took me to the most significant thing that ever happened in my lifetime," he finally said. "She's the one that took me there."

Barker is the chief of police in Indianapolis, Indiana.

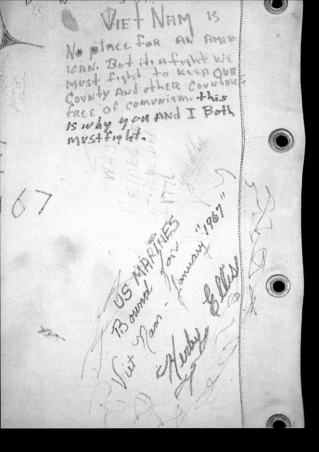

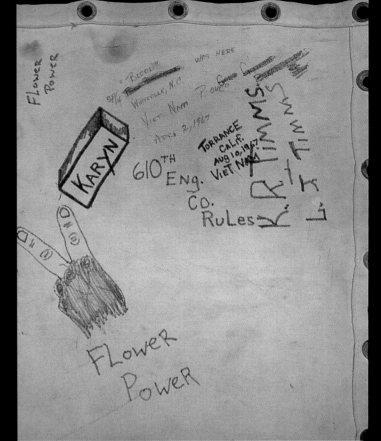

ABOVE In January 1967, a U.S. Marine, headed to war, recorded a reason why he felt Americans should fight in Vietnam.

TOP RIGHT A peace symbol was placed on this canvas—two extended fingers that formed a "V" and the words "Flower Power."

RIGHT One soldier couldn't wait to leave Vietnam, even before he got there. He inscribed on his canvas that he had only 350 days to serve in Vietnam, out of a one-year, 365-day duty tour. A soldier's tour of duty actually started the day the *Walker* left California.

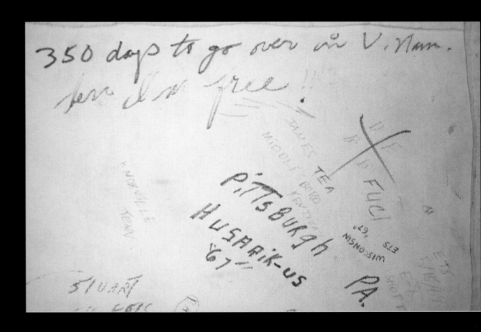

MR. MILITARY, ALL THE WAY

Garland "Skip" Whitmore was enjoying life as a Virginia Polytechnic Institute student in the summer of 1965.

He studied electrical engineering, entertained his classmates and friends with humorous impersonations, and played snare drum in the school's renowned "Highty-Tighty" band.

The young man was also concerned about the war in Vietnam and the spread of Communism, so he and classmate John Hoffnagle enlisted in the Army.

Whitmore excelled in training, and decided to make the military his career as an officer in the 1st Cavalry Squadron, 1st Cavalry Regiment. "He fell in love with the military," his father, G. Don Whitmore, of Harrisonburg, Virginia, recalled. Hoffnagle remembered, "He definitely was Mr. Military, all the way."

Second Lieutenant Whitmore stood squared away at the *Walker*'s railing during her August 1967 voyage to Vietnam. As an officer, he shared a cabin (similar to the one in the photo below, also on the *Walker*) with five other lieutenants, including Jim Lindsey.

The ship's public address system continuously barked maritime orders, primarily to the crew, Lindsey recalled. "We had listened to all this nautical stuff and didn't know what it meant," he said. "He [Whitmore] would mimic the announcements and all the jargon in a Donald Duck voice. It was quite humorous."

On August 28 the *Walker* arrived in Vietnam. On September 5, near Chu Lai, Lieutenant Whitmore was killed by fragments from an enemy mortar round.

(G. Don Whitmore and Charles Milford photos)

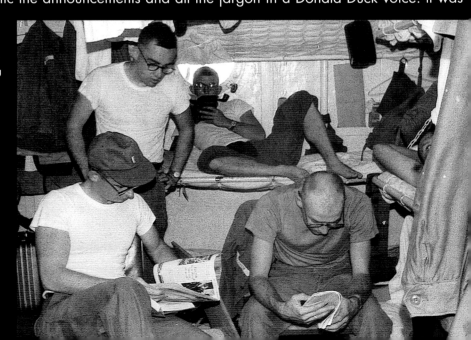

NAUTICAL TERMS

Found aboard the *General Nelson M. Walker* during our trips to the decaying ship was a 1960s directive that included a "GLOSSARY OF NAUTICAL TERMS" for passenger troops who might not be familiar with maritime terms used by the crew during a voyage. This is the complete glossary as it appeared in the directive.

AFT—Near, toward, or in the stern of the ship.

ALOFT—Refers to the general area above the ship's highest solid structure, i.e., the mastheads, topmasts, and the upper parts of the stacks, etc.

AMIDSHIP—Middle of ship's hull.

ASTERN—Expresses the idea of "directly behind the ship."

ATHWART—Expresses the idea of "across."

ATHWARTSHIPS—Direction at right angles to the center line of the ship.

BALLAST—Solids or liquids loaded into a ship for the purpose of increasing stability.

BATTEN DOWN HATCHES—To fasten hatch covers securely prior to sailing.

BEAM—Extreme width of ship.

BELOW DECKS—Refers to the general area below the main deck.

BILGE—The turn of the hull below the water line. Area of ship on inside near the keel.

BILGE KEELS—Keels at the turn of the bilge to offer resistance to the rolling motion of the ship.

BILGE PUMP—A pump for removing bilge water.

BILGE WATER—The foul water that collects in the bilge.

BITTS—A pair of wooden or iron heads on a ship set vertically to which mooring or towing lines are made fast.

BOAT—A ship which is capable of being carried on another ship.

BOW—Forward part of a ship.

BRIDGE—A high transverse platform extending from side to side of the ship, and from which a good view of the weather deck may be had. An enclosed space called the pilot house is erected on the bridge in which are installed the navigating instruments, such as the compass and binnacle, the control for the steering apparatus, and the signals to the engine room. The operation of the ship is directed from the bridge.

BRIG—Term applied to any compartment used for confinement of prisoners.

BROW—A gangplank, usually fitted with rollers at the end resting on the wharf to allow for the movement of the vessel with the tide.

BULKHEAD—One of the vertical partitions defining a compartment. Never called a wall.

BUNK—Sleeping accommodation. Never called a bed.

BUNKERS—Compartments of a ship in which fuel is carried; hence bunkering implies filling bunkers with fuel.

CHARTHOUSE—Compartment which contains the charts and other navigational equipment.

CHOCK—An iron casting which serves as a lead for lines to wharf or other ship.

COMPANIONWAY—Deck opening giving access to a ladder.

COMPARTMENT—An interior space defined by bulkheads.

CROSSING THE LINE—The act of crossing the equator.

CROW'S NEST—Lookout station aloft.

DAVITS—A pair of small cranes or radial arms on a ship's side for hoisting boats, stores, etc.

DECK—Horizontal planking or plating which divides a ship into layers of compartments. Never called a floor.

BOAT DECK—Deck where boats are carried.

MAIN DECK—The topmost deck extending to the hull at all points.

DOORWAY—Any opening through a bulkhead designed to accommodate human passage.

DRAFT—The depth of the keel.

FANTAIL—The after end of the main deck.

FATHOM—Six feet; a mariner's measure of depth.

FENDER—A device which acts as a buffer between ship and wharf.

FORE AND AFT—Direction parallel to the center line. Also expresses the idea of "the entire length of" or "both forward and aft."

FORE—Front of the ship.

FORWARD—Direction toward the bow.

FRAME—The part of a ship's framing which corresponds to the rib of a human skeleton.

FREEBOARD—The distance from the waterline to the top of the hull.

GALLEY—Ship's cooking compartment.

GANGWAY—Same as gangplank. Also used to designate deck area in immediate vicinity of ship end of gangplank.

GEAR—Expresses the idea of "equipment" or "apparatus."

HATCH—One of the large square openings in the deck of a ship through which freight is hoisted in or out. Also any opening through a deck designed to accommodate human passage.

HEAD—Officers' or crew's toilet.

HELM—Strictly speaking, a tiller. Actually the term (except as in "HELMSMAN") is seldom used on Navy ships, because of an inherent ambiguity. See RUDDER and WHEEL.

HOLD—Inside space below the lowest complete deck in which cargo is stowed.

HULL—The frame or body of a ship, not including its mastings, rigging, etc.

INBOARD—Toward the centerline.

KEEL—The large fore and aft steel structure at the bottom of a ship to which the frames are attached.

KNOT—A unit of speed, equivalent to one nautical mile per hour; as when a ship goes eight nautical miles an hour, her speed is eight knots. "Knots per hour" is incorrect.

LADDER—Any conventional ladder, or shipboard flight of steps. There are no "stairs" on a ship.

LEESIDE—The side of a ship protected from the wind.

LIST—Inclination or tilting of ship to one side, usually caused by unequal distribution of weight in the ship.

LOCKER—A storage compartment of a ship.

LOG—Book in which the watch officers record various data and all important events affecting the ship, her crew, and her passengers.

MESS—Eat. Also applies to the organization and facilities of messing.

MIND YOUR RUDDER—Steer more carefully.

NAUTICAL MILE—The sixtieth part of an equatorial degee, equal to 1852 meters or 6076.103 feet; therefore, 6 nautical miles represents approximately seven land miles.

OUTBOARD—"Away from the center line."

OVERHEAD—The ceiling.

PASSAGEWAY—A hall, corridor, or access area in a ship.

P/A SYSTEM—Public address system.

PORTHOLE—An exterior window, equipped with a means for water-tight closure.

PORT SIDE—The left side (red running light) of a ship looking forward.

QUARTERS—Expresses the general idea of "stations for a particular drill or maneuver." Also applied to living accommodations.

RIGGING—Terms for lines and/or wires which support a ship's masts, stacks, yards, etc., and the line, wires, and tackles which hoist, lower, and otherwise control the motion of the ship's movable deck gear.

RUDDER—A submerged vane attached to the stern which controls a ship's direction of travel. Incorporated in standard commands to helmsman, as in "Right full rudder."

SALOON—Dining room.

SCUTTLEBUTT—Drinking fountain. Also, rumor.

SECURE—Expresses the idea "to fix," "to attach," or "to make fast."

SHELL—The outside plating of a ship.

SHIP—Any ship which cannot be hoisted on board another ship.

STARBOARD SIDE—The right side (green running light) of a ship looking forward.

STEM—The bow extremity, also the structural member forming the point of the bow.

STERN—The aft or rear end of a ship

SUPERSTRUCTURE—Any structure built above the main deck, such as a deck house, bridge, etc.

TOPSIDE—Refers to the general area above the main deck.

TRACK—Proposed or actual path of a ship.

TURN IN—Go to bed.

UNDERWAY—Status of ship which is not attached to land (or the sea-bottom) in any way.

WAKE—The trail of disturbed water left by a moving ship.

WAY ON—A ship under way which is moving through water has "Way on," either "headway" or "sternway."

WEATHER DECK—Any deck area not protected by a roofed enclosure.

WEATHER SIDE—The side of a ship exposed to the wind.

WHEEL—Steering wheel of a ship.